URBAN CHRIST

Responses to
JOHN J VINCENT

Edited by
IAN K DUFFIELD

URBAN THEOLOGY UNIT

(c) Copyright Urban Theology Unit 1997
First published 1997

ISBN. 0.907490.11.5

Urban Theology Unit is Registered Charity No. 505334

All rights reserved. No part of this publication may be reproduced or transmitted in any form or by any means, electronic or mechanical, including photocopy, recording or any information storage and retrieval system without permission in writing from the holders of copyright to the material included.

URBAN THEOLOGY UNIT
210 Abbeyfield Road
Sheffield
S4 7AZ

Typeset by Anne Lewis and Kathy Bhogal at the Urban Theology Unit.

Printed by Tartan Press, Attercliffe, Sheffield

CONTENTS

Contributors		4
Introduction	Ian K Duffield	6
DISCIPLESHIP		9
Discipleship as Centre	Elizabeth Mitchell	10
THEOLOGY		14
Doing Urban Theology	Ian K Duffield	15
JESUS		24
The Jesus of the Inner City	Laurie Green	25
GOSPEL		34
Journey Downwards	Chris Rowland	35
STORY-MAKING		47
Towards an Urban Hermeneutics	Andrew Davey	47
DYNAMICS		53
Gospel Patterns	Robin Pagan	53
POLITICS		66
A Political Christ?	Alan Billings	67
MISSION		77
The Christ of Urban Mission	Colin Marchant	78
John James Vincent		
Bibliography		83
Biography		90
UTU Publications		92

CONTRIBUTORS

ALAN BILLINGS is Rector of St George's Kendal, formerly Director of the West Midlands Ministerial Training Scheme and a Member of the Faith in the City Commission (1985). He completed his DMin at New York Theological Seminary, through UTU, in 1987. He is a part-time tutor on the MMin/DMin of UTU/Sheffield University.

ANDREW DAVEY is the Anglican Bishops' Officer for Urban Priority Areas, in Church House, London. Previously a vicar in North Peckham, he is a 1983 UTU Study Year graduate, and wrote "Being Church as Political Praxis" in Liberation Theology UK. He is currently completing his UTU/Sheffield University MMin/DMin.

IAN K DUFFIELD is Vicar of St Mary's, Walkley, Sheffield and Vice Chair of the Diocesan Faith in the City Committee. He completed his NYTS DMin in 1984. He has been a lecturer at UTU since 1985, and is from 1997, Supervisor of the MMin/DMin course. The first volume of his Radical Voices in the Bible is expected in 1998.

LAURIE GREEN is Bishop of Bradwell in the Chelmsford Diocese. Formerly he was Principal of the Aston Training Scheme. He completed his NYTS DMin in 1983. He was a part-time lecturer at UTU, 1982-84 and currently is one of its Honorary Lecturers. UTU publishes his God in the Inner City and a 1997 booklet on Jubilee.

COLIN MARCHANT is a Baptist Urban Missioner, who has worked in the East End for many years, where he was Warden of Laurence Hall. He was President of the Baptist Assembly of Great Britain in 1989-90. He wrote Signs in the City in 1985, and his history of Urban Mission in Britain is forthcoming.

ELIZABETH MITCHELL is currently a part-time tutor with the West Midlands Ministerial Training Scheme and a Methodist Local Preacher. She did the UTU Study Year part-time 1983-87, and was a part-time Lecturer at UTU, 1992-96, and is now Chair of the Methodist Student Ministers' Pastoral Oversight Committee and an Honorary Lecturer.

ROBIN PAGAN is Minister of the United Reformed Church at Northwood Hills, Pinner. He completed his NYTS DMin in 1984, joined the UTU/Sheffield MMin/DMin teaching staff in 1994 as a Lecturer and Core Staff member, and is from 1997 Associate Supervisor of the MMin/DMin Course.

CHRIS ROWLAND is Professor of New Testament Theology in Oxford University. An Honorary Lecturer at UTU, he is Joint Editor with John Vincent of the British Liberation Theology Series. Books include, Christian Origins, Radical Christianity, and the Revelation Commentary in the Epworth Series.

NOTE

Books and Articles by John Vincent are usually cited in summary form, with short title, date and page reference. Reference should be made to the Bibliography for further details, under the year given.

INTRODUCTION

IAN K DUFFIELD

The retirement of Rev Dr John J Vincent as Director of the Urban Theology Unit in Sheffield --which he founded, pioneered, and established as an alternative place for theological education and ministerial training (clergy and lay, black and white, men and women) -- is an appropriate time to issue this volume of essays.

In a way this participates in the European academic tradition of the **Festschrift**, in which fellow scholars honour one of their number. It may seem curious for the Urban Theology Unit, of all places, to be sponsoring such an "alien" tradition. But this volume is not strictly speaking a collection of academic essays (e.g. Colin Marchant), and is certainly not a sycophantic offering (e.g. Alan Billings), or an excuse for writers to trot out their latest thesis or idea (e.g. Elizabeth Mitchell). It is more a collection of pieces especially written by friends and colleagues of John who have all benefited in one way or another from John's distinctive ministry, teaching, and provocation.

In this volume we have asked for responses to what John has said and done in a way that will stimulate further dialogue. This is an attempt, by some of us who have known John over the years, to respond more or less directly to what he has written in both book and article. It varies from Robin Pagan's very detailed examination of John's use of Gospel Patterns, through Bishop Laurie Green's questioning piece which likens John Vincent to John the Baptist, to Alan Billings' attack on John's supposed Christian egalitarian socialism! As you will discover, the people who have written are not prone to idolize others, and are not slow to be critical or to voice their own perceptions. These essays are written by practitioners of liberation theology (e.g. Professor Chris Rowland), working ministers (e.g. Rev Robin Pagan) and Bishops (Laurie Green), former students (most of us), theological colleagues (e.g. Rev Andrew Davey), UTU staff members (e.g. Ian K Duffield), fellow trainers (e.g. Elizabeth Mitchell), and activists (e.g. Colin Marchant) in the midst of their active engagement, and I am grateful for their ready and willing response to the invitation to be involved in this tribute to John Vincent.

The contributors who appear in this volume represent various traditions and styles, but nevertheless are not completely representative of all the members of UTU or participants on courses who embrace a far greater range. Indeed, the number of us who are Anglicans writing in this volume about a Methodist Minister will doubtless surprise many within Methodism as well as the Church of England. But at least it testifies to the significance of UTU and John's work that it cannot neatly be labelled 'Methodist'. After all, UTU as John set it up is an ecumenical body in terms of its basis, staffing, participants, and membership, and furthermore is a unit within another of John's creations: SICEM (Sheffield Inner City Ecumenical Mission).

John sees himself as a disciple, and Elizabeth Mitchell's essay highlights that with John you know "that the teaching and the writing are coming out of the living". Andrew Davey deals with John's urban hermeneutics and the significance of both stories and context: "The place is the arena of the story". This significance of location is picked up also in Ian Duffield's offering as he seeks to explain the dialectical method or process of doing urban theology which John advocates which leads to action. Robin Pagan provides us with a detailed examination and analysis of the patterns and dynamics of the gospel narrative as it has been articulated throughout all of John's writing years, and suggests some constructive improvements.

Chris Rowland speaks of his own experience of place in Brazil which has affected him as a theologian and enabled him to relate to John's agenda. He testifies that John's pioneering role in persistently advocating "an option for the inner city and the role of context in theology, has been indispensable in transforming theological education in these islands". In contrast, Alan Billings' contribution, which acknowledges his debt to John for helping him to think and re-think, implies that John is a member of a dying breed called 'egalitarian socialist', which reflects Alan's own re-thinking about politics and socialism over recent years.

From Laurie Green's new location as Bishop, he suggests, provocatively, that there are others alongside the inner city poor who may have a hermeneutical advantage, namely, those who thought they had made it. Colin Marchant, our Baptist contributor who has journeyed with John in both national and international circles including the first World Congress of Urban Mission, evokes through hymn and rhythm some of the power of John's convictions and commitments to the Christ of Urban Mission and the need to earth the Gospel.

John's writing has been largely done 'on the run' in the midst of active service, and we hope in 'retirement' as he refuses 'to sit down', as Methodism quaintly describes it, that he will produce more extended and detailed reflections on his vast experience and creative theologizing from within the context of the inner city (see, for example, Ian K Duffield's essay).

These essays are a preliminary look and taking stock of John's writing and contribution to date with some analysis or assessment, and indeed provocation for more. It will be clear that as friends, colleagues -- ever disciples, some of us -- we do not always agree with him. There is a healthy debate going on and this volume reflects part of that debate as a few of us respond to John Vincent. But hopefully we do so in a way which honours what John has tried to do. His writing is significant, even if somewhat elusive at times, and to this we bear witness.

An attempt has been made to provide a reasonably comprehensive bibliography of John's writings, which will be of interest to many. A number of these writings are referred to in the essays in this volume, although it has obviously not proved possible or practical to cover all that John has written or done. In addition we have provided some extracts from John's writings to set alongside the essays that have been written to cover some of the width of John's concerns, interests, and activity. Some of that width is encompassed in our title, Urban Christ, because at the end of the day, it has been these twin concerns, reference points, and 'loves' that say so much about John Vincent, his thought, and his work.

September 1997 marks a turning point with a new role for John and for others of us. All of us now look to the future of the Urban Theology Unit with Inderjit Bhogal as Director, as we seek to remain true to the original vision. That will be to ensure that both Christ and the Urban - and their mutual engagement - are kept high on the agenda of the Urban Theology Unit into the new millenium.

IAN K DUFFIELD

Walkley
July 1997

DISCIPLESHIP

The heart of Mark's Gospel is that people now can follow. They can follow because there are twelve, or more or less, people cluttering the way behind the hero. And since the twelve appear so dumb, then at least there is room in the church for the most unlikely fellow-traveller in the Way. People now can follow, because the whole of the Gospel is a story that never has a beginning or an end - or, rather, is repeatedly having beginnings and endings, as generation after generation - or at least new disciple after new disciple - gets caught up in the good news about Jesus the Messiah. The call to discipleship says: "It's starting - get with it!" And by the end, it is not the end, but "So you're still here - Get back to the start again". The "eschatological perspective" is simply that it is always the end and the beginning for some part of the action, and some part of the Church. It is always some individual's "beginning", as they hear the call to discipleship (Mk.1), and some individual's "end" as they face fiery trial, rejection, or persecution (Mk. 13).

Discipleship sets us at the very centre of the mystery of the New Testament. It sets us at the centre of the New Testament, because it sets us, naturally, artlessly, without explanation or justification, in the midst of the action behind the documents - the action whereby human beings are caught up into relationship to another human being, in whom is understood to be, and discovered by some to be, all the secrets of existence. In Mark the disciples are discipled to Jesus, and Jesus is discipled to the Kingdom, and the Kingdom replaces Torah as the synonym or the surrogate for God.

The Church of Mark was a "discipleship" church. It knows nothing of hierarchies. The Gospel of Mark sees the purpose of existence not as faithful adherence to the teaching and the teaching authority (as in Matthew), or in faithful waiting for the kerygmatic salvation-events (as in Luke), but rather in faithful action - involvement in the dynamic event of Jesus. If the Gospel was written for Church lections (as the form critics claimed), then it was for a Church which saw its joy and its salvation in the constant and recurring judgement and mercy, acceptance and rejection, invitation and repulsion, faith and unfaith, following and fleeing, crucifying and rising which is the story of the "Good Master", and also the story of his disciples. That the twelve numbered more or less at various times, is apparently without dogmatic significance. But it is with thoroughgoing dogmatic intention that the twelve are there, doing it all, or not doing it all. It is Mark's whole theology that the twelve are the exemplars and typical initiators of that whole incessant drama whereby in human existence anyone following this Jesus is always successively and dramatically under judgement and under mercy, successively accepted and rejected, successively being invited and repulsed, successively in faith and in unfaith, successively following and forsaking, successively crucified and rising. The church that sat hearing Mark's Gospel no more knew whether to laugh or cry than did the twelve, no more knew whether they would be "in at the kill" than did the twelve, no more knew when "the day or the hour" would be than did the twelve, no more knew whether they would "stay with him" through the persecution-cross than did the twelve. Thus is the Church of Mark a "discipleship" church: a church existing alongside and within that singular existence that people have when the one who has become "lord and master" is present as the "way" which disciples and disciple-community "follow".

Disciple and Lord, 1976, pp 117-118

DISCIPLESHIP AS CENTRE

ELIZABETH MITCHELL

Responding positively to the invitation to write this piece provided a reason to re-visit some of the books added to the shelves in the last 30 years - and to recall some formative moments of excitement, encouragement and challenge from the writings of John Vincent.

The presentation of *discipleship* as centre offered a life-line to those of us who were floundering with God questions in the 1960s. We didn't know whether there was anything we could say about God. We didn't know whether there was a God about whom anything could be said. yet the figure of Jesus remained strangely attractive, tantalising and mysterious. Yet provocative. And here came a suggestion that what we needed was simply to put our feet in his direction - to follow, to become disciples, to have a go at participating in his actions - and let the God questions sort themselves out as we engaged in this.

John Vincent has a memorable picture of the pattern of discipleship, as presented in St Mark's Gospel, being "feet, then stomach, then heart, then head". The disciples first tread the path that Jesus takes; they eat with him (and the motley crew he seems to choose to have meals with); they begin to love him - and then, maybe they have a glimpse of understanding. For me, who thought I needed to have some clear conceptual grasp of who Jesus was and what he was about and how I might be in relationship with him, before being able to commit myself to action, this came as a challenge and as a comfort. There were precedents from the beginning for walking with him without being sure what it was all about!

It was interesting that while I was preparing this material, I heard a lecture by Karen Armstrong, entitled "Has God a Future?"[1] It was based on her research into the development of the three major monotheistic religions, and she pointed out that all the pioneers in these traditions have said that it's no good trying to prove satisfactorily the existence and nature of God, and then live in the light of that. Rather, they have all said that first you must step into the unknown; take the risk of adopting the disciplines of a particular lifestyle - then you'll know.

The disciplines of the life-style to which Jesus called people - characterised by John Vincent in the phrases "a journey backwards, a journey sideways, a journey downwards" - resonate with those in late 20th century Western society who ask themselves how they might live their lives without shutting their eyes to the economic, environmental and ecological concerns of this present age. Some of the slogans, "The personal is the political" and "Small is beautiful", seem to have Gospel echoes. Many "alternative" lifestyles have been on offer - and in this post-modern, pluralistic culture, the "Jesus Thing" can stand alongside the rest. Perhaps what makes it most distinctive is that the likelihood of failure is built into the model.

In more recent years, I have been working with Jung's theory of psychological type, and have found myself reflecting, in terms of that particular way of looking at humanity, about who is most likely to respond to presenting discipleship as centre. Because it is an approach which is earthed and practical and about doing something in the world, it will immediately connect with the type of which there seems to be a majority in the population. [2] For those, like me, who are more at home in the inner world of ideas and concepts, who want to see the grand plan, the future goal,[3] it comes as a necessary provocation to actually get on and do something! Among the people who have come and joined the Study Year at UTU, we have had far more of the latter group than the former. One has been able to observe over the years how focussing on discipleship has been a key, opening a door for people to risk taking a step towards making their visions become reality. The question then becomes one of finding the lifestyle which can support the action, allowing the appropriate space (which introverts especially need) for reflection and re-creation.

One of my continuing concerns has been the encouraging and development of lay ministry. I have discovered that "discipleship" thinking and language is often very releasing to people, freeing them to take initiatives or enabling them to recognise that some of the things they are already about in their secular lives are as significant for the Kingdom as what they may do as church officers, and so be more confident. It is also important in fostering an attitude which sees it as acceptable not to know everything, not to get things right always and to need to go on learning.

As I have worked with women's groups, I have been pushed to a re-evaluation of the picture of discipleship in the Gospels, and the paradigm which John Vincent draws out, particularly from Mark. The marginalisation of the women disciples by the Gospel writer [4] means that for many women now the word "disciple" evokes a male image with which they find it hard to identify. We have looked for the hidden women of the gospel story, and realised that as well as the ones eventually mentioned, who travelled with Jesus, so there are many, on whom the mission has depended, who have stayed at home, providing hospitality and meals for those who have come proclaiming the good news, looking after the children the men have left behind, and obviously there in the groups that have gathered around to listen to Jesus, affirmed in his words "Whoever does the will of God is my brother and my sister and my mother." [5] We have also realised that one of the things which the twelve male disciples are portrayed as having to learn - to serve[6] - is done spontaneously by women.[7] Women who suspect this is simply keeping them in their proper place in a patriarchy, are encouraged by the stories of Jesus' affirmative response to women breaking the taboos of their culture and behaving assertively.[8] In her commentary on Mark's gospel, Joanna Dewey writes that "within the narrative world, Mark uses women and their behaviour to model for men the true nature of discipleship".[9] So, despite all the difficulties "discipleship" has still offered a way of accessing the text, provoking useful questions about it, and inviting people to "change yourselves completely and trust yourselves to the Good News."[10]

I do wonder about those for whom "discipleship" might not offer a way in. How does "Give up everything; come and follow me" sound when you are constrained by physical and mental handicaps, by illness, by age, by responsibilities for the care of others? Is everyone called to be a disciple? John Vincent does imply, at points, that all of the Gospel is not for all of the people all of the time. He also says that it is important to go positively with what is for you, rather than using negatives to dismiss the whole challenge.

I was working with John on the "Discipleship" module in the Study Year, during the period I was thinking about how to write this piece. It was not the first occasion I had shared in this process, and I was struck again by how each time John himself makes some new discovery about the picture of discipleship in Mark's Gospel. Each time, in the interaction with others engaging with the material, bringing their life experience, fresh insights come. And the students have the example of one who is constantly doing what we are encouraging them to do: to put themselves in the disciple place and find out what it means. All the time one knows that the teaching and the writing are coming out of the living, and that is the great strength of the work.

---

1. Loughborough University Annual Chaplaincy Lecture 1997
2. The Extraverted Sensing type, for those who are familiar with the jargon.
3. The Introverted Intuitive
4. We suddenly hear in the penultimate chapter that there have been women who have followed and served Jesus in Galilee and come up to Jerusalem with him!
5. Mark 3: 35
6. Mark 10: 35-45
7. Mark 1: 31 and Mark 15: 41
8. Mark 5: 25-34 and Mark 7: 24-30
9. In *Searching the Scriptures*, Vol. 2, ed Elisabeth Schussler Fiorenza
10. Mark 1: 15 (JV customary translation)

THEOLOGY

The question now arises: What does it mean for the interpretor of scripture to "work at the Word" in the context of contemporary urban existence? What does it mean to read the stories of Israel's attempts to discover political liberation, or ethnic recognition, or internal justice, or wholeness for all, from among and alongside those who live contemporary history with similar agendas?

No task is of greater importance than to apply the rigour of socio-historical disciplines now among the contemporary hearers and doers of the Word, as we have learned to apply them to the creators of the Word itself. Put bluntly - does not the still persisting, educated, suburban, and sophisticated captivity of the Word mean that a fundamental dissonance is set up, if those who attempt today to study the Word stand diametrically opposed, in the corresponding social, economic, and political positions of our day, to those who originally created the stories and the records, among whom the "acts of God" took place, and within whose contexts and concerns the very truths and assumptions that we today distil and use for other purposes originally came to birth? .....

My own journey had taken me through New Testament studies to urban mission and eventually into urban theology. Early, I became convinced that discipleship rather than belief was the essence of Christianity. In 1954-55, I pursued this prejudice in a year at Drew Theological Seminary (Madison, NJ) and wrote my conclusions. Oscar Cullmann visited Drew, and I got to Basel for a year, where I worked on discipleship, mainly in Mark's Gospel.

Three conclusions followed my enthusiasm. First, that you could not really get a doctorate out of discipleship without yourself being prepared to go in for it. Second, that the way of the disciple could only be carried out in a practical commitment of a specific and alternative kind. I remember saying to myself that "I need to find a place where Gospel things might happen." It was not that I would be the originator of gospel things, but that I would be part of them. The third conclusion followed from this: The nearest place to being where Jesus was in his own lifetime was to put myself in one of the great cities. So being a disciple for me meant being a city missioner. My institutional creations twenty years ago followed. Because the inner city was being deserted by the Christians, I helped form the Sheffield Inner City Ecumenical Mission, And as no one knew how to be a theologian there, I started UTU.

So, I want to know not simply what places in the gospel can help me with my place and vocation in the city, but even more, what disciplines and vocations, practice and spirituality, I now as an inner-city person need to be open to in order that the gospel may happen around me; that is, in order that I can also fulfil my vocation as a New Testament student and a theologian in my vocation, in the inner city.

"Mark's Gospel in the Inner City", 1991, pp. 275-277

DOING URBAN THEOLOGY

IAN K DUFFIELD

What does it mean to be a theologian in the context of modern Britain, living in a poor multi-racial area in a major city, radicalized by the gap between rich and poor? For John Vincent it has meant an incarnational ministry within Sheffield's inner city (Into the City, 1982), a training ministry towards clergy and laity for work alongside the poor (Alternative Theological Education, 'Training for Ministry at the Urban Theology Unit', 1994), and being an urban theologian (Into the City 1982 'Towards an Urban Theology', 1983, 'Doing Theology' in Agenda for Prophets, 1980).

Urban theology is doing theology in the context of the urban. For John Vincent this has also meant doing political theology as he has engaged with major political and social issues such as nuclear disarmament (Christ in a Nuclear World , 1962; Christian Nuclear Perspective, 1964; 'The Way Ahead: Between Protest and Politics', 1966); and racism (The Race Race, 1969; Britain in the 90's, 1989, ch.5). He has also campaigned against the change of status of the

TSB (1986). Increasingly, the issues that have dominated him in the last fifteen years or so have been those of urban policy and urban affairs (Two Nations -- One Gospel ,1981; Britain in the 90's, 1989; Petition of Distress from the Cities, 1993; The Cities, 1997).

For urban theology to be done, the urban and theology must meet and engage. A crucible is required to mix the ingredients; secular elements and elements from the "theological storehouse". Urban theology is inevitably contextual theology--but then so is every theology in reality, even if people are blind to it;

> There never has been any writer of Scripture or writer of theology whose vision and message were not addressed to the context of the day, which means determined and shaped by the political, economic and cultural situation of the time and place in which the writer was living. (Agenda for Prophets, p.127).

Theology needs primarily to be done not in the Church (as one of John's theological heroes, Karl Barth, advocated) or in the University (where no doubt John himself would have become a Professor of New Testament), but in the City. Theology for him has to be, therefore, urban theology. Indeed, John Vincent has established himself, over the last twenty five years, as the leading exponent of urban theology within Britain. This theology is not safe or tame, and people get scandalized by it. John knows this. The quotation he placed at the front of Secular Christ (1968), from an editorial on the theologian Paul Tillich, proclaimed:

"There is no such thing as a 'safe' theology.
All theology which is earnest is also dangerous.
It is an act of adoration, fraught with the risk of blasphemy."

John clearly answers the question 'Where is theology done?' in terms of the inner city and urban realities (note Chris Rowland's essay in this volume). The context or location in which theological reflection takes place is so important, for we are all so dependent upon where we stand, and who we stand with. Location is decisive ('Liberation Theology and the Practice of Ministry", 1992 p.5), because:"Every theology is determined by its context (p. 4) or as he has said more recently: "All theology is, and has always been, contextual. (Liberation Theology UK, 1995, p.18). So John is inevitably, but also self-consciously, an urban theologian.

Theology always begins with location. It is within a particular context and experience that theological reflection takes place and is moulded into shape. In Britain that dominating location is the urban, whether people live in cities or not. So in a general sense everyone who calls themselves a theologian in Britain is an urban theologian. However, because so many submit to the suburban or middle class captivity of theology (Liberation Theology UK, 1995, p.17f), it is those who live, work, and act on the raw edge of the urban reality who are in the most privileged context for doing theology.

Thus theology has to be done from 'bottom"--and not from the top or the middle--with and alongside the poor. Urban theology cannot be done by those who will not accept the location and the dangers it poses. It is 'boundary theology' for it is done on the boundary, on the margins of life. If we define the location more precisely, it is the boundary between rich and poor, between church and non-church, between indigenous and migrant, between employed and unemployed, between local communities and political parties, between people and bureaucracies. To say that urban theology is 'boundary theology' is not to imply a tight-rope walking act, or a neutral theology. It is to say that the realities of the urban are most clearly seen in the interfaces between rich and poor, and so on. Urban theology has its location amongst the poor, the people, and local communities, although it is never submerged by them. It has to walk the boundary and face realities from their perspective, from the bottom. John has consistently and urgently proclaimed the importance and significance of location. In one of John's well known phrases, 'Where You Are Is Who You Are' (Liberation Theology UK, 1995 p.18). He has persistently called people to move to the inner city, to see discipleship as entailing living and working alongside the poor, to accept the challenge of the Gospel to take the journey backwards, sideways, or downwards (Alternative Journeys, 1981; Into the City, 1982, p.110ff). The urban theologian, like the liberation theologian, has to have "the will to stand alongside and learn from the poor". (OK, Let's be Methodists, 1984 p. 68).

John frequently uses the theological term of incarnation to convey particularity and the importance of location (Into the City, Ch.1; Strategies for Mission, 1976 p2f). "Any Christian Ministry has to begin with incarnation, a radical taking seriously of some part of the human situation. ('Liberation Theology and the Practice of Ministry", 1992 p.10). If ministry begins with incarnation, so too does theology. For John himself this has been a matter of vocation;

a call to live, work, minister, and do theology in the inner city. It is a self-chosen, intentional locating for being a disciple, a New Testament scholar and a theologian. This is why so many others fail to be urban theologians; they do not seek a base at the bottom, they do not see the significance of the social, economic and cultural forces at work around them, they do not intentionally do urban theology. Urban theology is no casual reflecting on the Christian tradition, but rather a radical call from God to reflect with the people in the midst of decay and despair upon the realities of their situation and what the Gospel says to it. Although, sadly, it still needs defending, the context of the urban poor is a legitimate place from which to do theology (Liberation Theology UK, 1995, p.19f).

Anyone who has been on any of our courses at UTU will at some point hear John say: 'You, are your own best theologian' as a way of affirming the reflective task that we all have to engage in, and the wisdom of not being dependent upon another's thoughts. But John is quite clear that there are good and bad ways of going about the task of being a theologian. Where you do the task of theologizing is one critical element, as we have seen, another is the process whereby elements of the Christian faith, or the 'theological storehouse', connect with the concerns that are experienced:

"The true theologian says, 'How does the Gospel itself come newly to me, where I am, with my own questions and presuppositions--and to my people, those with whom I live, and move and have my being?" Agenda for Prophets, p.123)

Such reflective thinking that theology is, brings together and attempts to correlate the particular situation and struggle of the people now, with the words, action and vision of God's People in different places and other times. As John says of base communities, urban theology is "grass-roots, do-it-yourself, people-based", a reflection upon praxis (Basic Communities in Britain, 1980, p.59) Something has to be done, or experienced first. As Gutierrez has taught us, theology is the second act. John even calls it "the end-product of gospel faithfulness and secular commitment. (Into the City, p.117), because he assumes that you have to do something first as a disciple before you can do serious theology about it.

Long before most people had heard of Liberation Theology John had declared programmatically on the basis of the essays in Stirrings, (1976): "Theology arises from action " (p.109). For John, and all liberation theologians, theology does not begin with ideas but with happenings: "All theology, I claim, must be theology from the bottom. It must begin not with ideas--one's own or other people's--but with happenings. (OK, Let's be Methodists, 1984, p.65). Theology as a reflective response to what is happening entails listening and analysing carefully what is going on and then seeking to relate the Christian faith to that. As John also said long ago:

> "The theologian's task is ... to hear the stories actually being told out of the gospels and out of contemporary existence, and to tell them again with their theological significance more plainly shown." (Stirrings, p.109)

How you bring theology and context, gospel and situation, faith and reality together is the vital issue. But it is so difficult, and there is no one ready-made way to do it (Agenda for Prophets, p.131). At UTU we are constantly working at this process which we believe to be so vital. We know at least it entails a serious analytical engagement with the particularities and structures of a social situation at the same time as a deep entering into the dynamics of the Gospel (see Robin Pagan's essay in this volume). Unfortunately, people tend to focus on either one or the other and the dialogue that is necessary fails to take place. But doing urban theology requires that secular elements and Christian elements, situational 'bits' and theological 'bits', local stories and gospel stories are mixed and work on each other. It requires the making of "imaginative identifications", (Starting All Over Again, 1981, p.16; see also Mark at Work, 1986, and especially the recent article "Imaginative Identification", 1996) . This is a somewhat intuitive grasp of a deep connection between the contextual reality that is being faced and a part of the scriptural story. It is the discovery, or revelation, of a true resonance between the people of God in their contemporary struggles and the story of God's people in former times, as in every age disciples seek to be faithful to God's Project. John frequently offers his own 'identifications' from the synoptic gospels, but they are always meant to be "invitations and provocations to others to open the Gospels and make their own identifications",.(Starting All Over Again, p. 18).

If we look more closely at this fundamental theological method used by urban theology we find that it is a Method of Correlation. This method is employed by Paul Tillich in his theology (Systematic Theology), although for him it is relating theological answers to existential questions, where the questions tend to be personal and psychological. For urban theology such existential concerns and questions with ultimacy are seen within a social and communal context. The deep questions are forced upon us by social pressures, political struggles, economic forces, and our experiences-in-community. Theology is dialogue between these 'life and death' problems which arise out of our social existence and the Jewish-Christian tradition to which we belong--and especially for John the stories of Jesus (<u>Radical Jesus</u> and <u>Mark at Work</u>). There is a real dialogue, where the tradition is shaped by the actual experience, and the deep problems of communal existence are articulated in the light of religious tradition. Urban theologians need to embrace more clearly and consciously this dialogical, and even dialectical, method or process.

It is clear, therefore, that urban theology is not so much a set of doctrines as a process and a way of theologizing. Some will engage in this consciously and deliberately, but John obviously believes that sometimes the people themselves theologize unselfconsciously, and encourages us to recognize it happening in small urban communities:

> "'Urban theology' <u>appears</u>, when people in the context of the demands and opportunities, the limitations and determinisms of the city, affirm and tell their own stories, and find within the Gospel, elements which will help them affirm, fight and change their situation." (<u>Starting All Over Again</u>, p.16, my emphasis)

All the time John is trying to get urban theology to happen. Perhaps he is always 'starting all over again' (see Robin Pagan's essay), because for him such theology is a method and a process which he is always using in one form or another with congregations and groups. Consequently, it is always different every time, because there are different people, different contexts, and different stories. This means, unfortunately, that some of John's writing can seem very occasional, because he does appear to begin again and again. Only, perhaps, in <u>Into the City</u> is there a more sustained reflection and working through of the dialectic between contextual experiences and gospel paradigms. There is a need for John in the future to give us more extended treatments of urban theology so that the fruits of the method and the process can be more clearly seen and appreciated.

At UTU generally we have tended to be strong on situation analysis, but weaker on social or structural analysis. Asian Christians who have studied with us have been the first to highlight this weakness, and we need to respond even more to that challenge. Consequently, it would be good to see John engaging with an urban theology for the UK which addressed more fully the deep social and structural issues of the society in which we live. This would tie in with his recent involvement in the Methodist report The Cities (1997) and study material for it, and his call as President of the Methodist Conference to the nation: Britain in the 90's (1989).

Also at UTU we have tended to emphasize the gospel elements of Mark's Gospel, which is John's New Testament specialism, more than other biblical or doctrinal material. It would now be good for John to address more fully these other parts of the Christian storehouse with a view to their correlation with an urban theology for the UK. This would tie in with the British Liberation Theology Project of which Liberation Theology UK (1995) was the first volume where, for example, Chris Rowland makes use of Luke-Acts (p.48ff).

Another reason, perhaps, for John's apparent reluctance in the past to move much beyond glimpses at an urban theology method and its results, is that John is more concerned that others have a go at doing theology this way for themselves. Furthermore, he desires that something actually happens--that action take place-- rather than end up debating urban theology as a syllabus item. As he says of the study of the gospels, they open up in a totally new way when they are seen not as records to be debated so that I get it right in my head, but as living dynamics and actions to be entered into, even imitated, so that I get it right in my feet and hands! (Radical Jesus, 1986, p.96).

So, if theology arises from action, it also leads to action. You might even say, according to John, that the purpose of theology is action (Starting All Over Again p.17). Thus urban theology can be seen to be a branch or type of Liberation Theology, and very different from what many in the academy or church circles regard an theology. But theology that is rooted in urban realities will always move towards action, if only because it has come from action in the first place. Something has already happened, been experienced, struggled against, which has led to thinking, reflection, and hence theology. Urban theology thus assists the articulation of both understanding and response to the situation. Not understanding alone, as if we can really understand something, truly become aware, and then not act. To truly understand, to be fully aware, leads to action. Reflective contextual theology becomes a tool for the framing of action. John truly believes that the Gospel will provide fuel for action, a counter-cultural perspective, an antidote to ideological structures, and motivation towards transformation. This is a fundamental belief and assumption that he operates by. The Gospel is the great mystery for John and he hardly ever clarifies what he means by it because it functions as a great symbol, but there can be no doubt that he regards the Gospel as essentially liberating and liberative.

Urban theology is also a form of practical theology because it takes the current situation with all its complexities, structures, and ambiguity seriously, and begins to fashion relevant, practical and systemic action. That is why John has been insistent at UTU that we encourage ministers (lay and ordained), to engage in projects in ministry. A project approach to ministry is still new for many clergy, but this reflects John's own approach to ministry as in Into the City, and is fundamental to the Master of Ministry Degree Programme that John has helped pioneer in this country. Ministry projects focus on specific pieces of work in a particular context, they are framed to facilitate change or transformation in the light of the Gospel. An urban theology, which takes seriously the resonances between the particular situation and the corporate spiritual tradition and history to which we belong, can suggest alternative models, prophetic actions, acted parables, and spiritual resources for sustaining action. Thus urban theology in not so much written as done. It goes on whenever groups of Christians and others reflect on their situation and struggle in the light of their religious tradition, and live active and committed lives as a consequence of that reflection. Urban theology is thus a continuous activity and will be carried on differently in each particular situation as it takes the particularities of that place and its people seriously.

Back in Stirrings (p.107) John wondered what would happen if the Jesus of the synoptic gospels was the focus for the doing of theology, if it was all done from this point. He suggested that it would only be after more stories and irreconcilable Jesus-images that the theologian will be needed as a 'systematizer' (p.109). Twenty one years on, is this now what John Vincent needs to do? Perhaps, after all the projects, campaigns and activity, and all the experience of engaging in the method of urban theology with countless groups of people it is time to be more systematic. Thirty years ago John laid down some "Fragments for a New Theology." (Secular

Christ, Part Three). To those fragments need to be added the other fragments that John has distributed over the years. All of them now need to be collected into twelve baskets full and re-distributed!

For some years now John has lectured on 'A Christ-Centred Radical Dogmatics'. He has drawn impressive diagrams on the board whereby he has sought to make imaginative identifications, connections and correlations between elements of the fundamental human situation, the Gospel Storehouse, and the activity of Jesus Christ. It is time for this to come together. Because of his commitment we know it will be Christ-centred, because at heart John is simply a disciple of Jesus. But for John this Jesus is the Radical Jesus that he has discovered in the gospels, and therefore. inevitably it will be a Radical Dogmatics (Radical Jesus p.94). And because of all of John's commitments and campaigns over the years, we know that such a dogmatics will be related to the realities and problems of the world, especially urban life. Some kind of systematizing work is now needed from the person who has pioneered urban theology in this country and ceaselessly encouraged others to do it. There can be no doubt that a Radical Dogmatics from John Vincent would not only be a great gift to the Church, but also it would be an invitation and a provocation to others And if he got other people to do their own urban theology, or liberating systematics, or radical dogmatics, he would be pleased.

JESUS

There is another possibility: that Christianity begins by being "over against" the area of ordinary secular experience, but precisely because of what Christianity is, it shows quite specifically that the "dimension of depth and trust and hope" in the secular can be significant in so far as the Christological and revealed categories manifest themselves within the secular. That is, exactly what secular deeds are already "the works of Christ"? Christianity looks to Christ to discover the present Christ. The Christian is "involved" not because he is submerged, like everyone else, in the modern secular spirit, but because he knows what he is looking for - the marks of the ministry of Christ, the ministry of healing. Until this theological question is set right, we shall continue to flounder concerning what is and what is not the "Christian presence" amid contemporary humanism.

Let us seek to elaborate this a little further.

1. Christ's ministry is healing to the broken city (polis, politeia). Christ protests at the religious hypocrites of his day. But he weeps over the city. He supports the existing Roman social order. He "uses" the church now to continue his ministry to the world. The aim of the church is the redemption, salvation, healing, wholeness of the world, the politeia. So that the Christian's immediate commitment is to politics, not protest; to involvement, not exclusiveness; to dirty hands, not clean ones. Any other concept of discipleship is defective. God is using the Christians for the benefit of his purposes for the world.

2. Christ's Way is God's "Expedient" Way in politics. The aim is not to be right, but to save. The parables and teaching of Jesus show how God juggles with the most unlikely of situations and persons so that somehow his will is done and "all comes out well". Naturally, there is a sense in which God's expedient will for humanity is not to be identified with every human "argument of expediency". But the aim is the same. Christian "witness" is not for the sake of the Christian, but for the sake of the world, to "heal", "save" it. Immediately, this means that the Christian is not permitted acts which may indicate personal passionate concern but which alienate those who it is God's will that he/she should persuade to a better way. And if people in responsible positions are accustomed to disregarding moral considerations, then the Christian must show how the moral is not irrelevant but also even immediately and politically expedient. We thus do not need to develop a theology of involvement as if basically we began with something other. God's specific will and presence are always "involved" already.

3. Christ's Way is a Technique of Initiative. The Christian contribution begins and ends with an application of the "technique" of Christ: imaginative self-identification with the persons ("sinners") involved; healing of individuals or situations of conflict; unilateral initiative in goodness so that "good may come to many"; vicarious suffering for the good of many. The classic theology of the cross is thus the theology for Christian action.

The Christian lives by involvement, not principle, because this is the pattern of the incarnation. And the pattern of the incarnation is the way whereby politics, as well a person receives healing. There are, of course, many who will argue this position from non-Christian grounds. Only the person who is "involved" can be a reconciler - the person who is prepared to be "right in himself". The Christ who "became sin for us", yet remaining sinless, is the sufficient model for the Christian. And the whole pattern may sufficiently tell us that radical Christian action will only be heeded if it is accompanied by personal and political commitment within the vexed areas at issue.

"Between Protest and Politics", 1966, pp. 252-254

THE JESUS OF THE INNER CITY

LAURIE GREEN

Once when John Vincent was offering a series of training courses in the Midlands, the clergyman who was in charge of the funding arrangements for such enterprises 'phoned me to say that he felt that, despite the minimal cost, this would be an extravagance since, as he put it, "I don't think we've got anything to learn from John Vincent, have we?" I sensed in his tone a certain anxiety. The fact of the matter was that he himself had already learned a great deal from John Vincent's work but he dared not admit it, for if he did, then he would have to begin to act on it!

John Vincent has always reminded me of John the Baptist. Not the Baptist which comes to us from the Markan material so beloved of John Vincent, but the Baptist who storms at us from the 'Quelle' material in Matthew's and Luke's accounts.

> "You viper's brood! ...Bring forth fruits worthy of repentance and do not say to yourselves, We have Abraham to our father; for I say unto you, That God is able of these stones to raise up children unto Abraham." [Luke 3: 7-8]

How often the Church, like the Pharisees whom the Baptist addresses, relies upon its heritage as those who know about God and feel convinced that they are saved by virtue of their belief in him. John Vincent wants more. He wants a Church which is a loving federation of groups of willing disciples who have covenanted one with another to "bring forth fruits worthy of repentance," where repentance means having discovered a whole new Gospel way of seeing the world - from the bottom up.

So, is John a latter day John the Baptist? And if so, in charging us to concentrate on "bringing forth fruits," is he inspiring a religion of 'Good Works' rather than a religion of 'Faith'? Or perhaps he's not stuck with religion at all, but rather a way of being committed doers of the things of Jesus?

John Vincent came to the conclusion that the essence of faith was discipleship rather than belief as early as 1954 when studying at Drew Theological Seminary, and later at Basel. He remembers saying to himself, "I need to find a place where Gospel things might happen." It was not that he would be the originator of Gospel things, but that he would be part of them if he could just find the right spot. Then as now, John was first and foremost a New Testament scholar and his search for the place where Gospel things might happen was borne of his realisation that the hermeneutical problem was constantly getting in the way of people being able to hear the Good News or responding to it.

The problem was this. How could western, white, wealthy students of the Gospel text ever be able to get into the mind of the eastern, poor, first century people who recorded in the Gospels their experience of Jesus of Nazareth? The gulf of culture, time, privilege and class was simply too great. And this problem led to two equally problematical responses. The first was to come at the text as if it were 'out of context' - written in no-time and no-place. Then it would be possible to read into the text as much of our own context and twentieth-century mind-set as we wished. That 'eisegesis' had its place, said Vincent, as long as it was clear to all just what a liberty we were taking with the text when we did it The second response to the problem would be to 'abstractify' the Gospel text by assuming that it contained a contextualised truth which could be abstracted from it for all time. On this basis we would look for the abstract 'truth' that the original writers were trying to convey in their context and then put that into words from our own context and culture which would express approximately the same insight. Indeed that was how most scholars and preachers were operating.

But John Vincent was not happy with either path. He wanted to be very true to the original context and acknowledge how far we have come apart from it, and he certainly was not content either to psychologise the text as Walter Wink was prone to do, or to spiritualise the text as most clergy prefer. He began instead to seek out a way of gaining 'hermeneutical advantage' by locating himself in a place and among people who would more naturally resonate with what his studies were telling him about the text. His studies were now being taken forward at a rate of knots by the work of those researching scholars who were investigating the social, political and economic realities of Galilee in the time of Jesus. They were making it crystal clear that Galilee had been greatly influenced by a sophisticated, Hellenistic ethos. Even the smaller Galilean villages were bound into the international trade networks by way of the larger towns of the Empire, such as Tiberias, Capernaum, Bethsaida-Julias and Kafar Hananiah. Just as it is today, Galilee had the feel of what today we call 'urban shadow'. But Vincent went further in his discoveries. For he already knew from his own experience of ministry that there were certain people today who have an instinctive sense of identification with the text of the Gospel and they had already given him insight into its meaning. This natural empathy was to be found in our time among the poor of the inner city.

Of course there were limitations in the correspondence between first century Galilee and the inner cities of our day, but the similarities of experience for the poor in both contexts were profound. As John Vincent continued to explore, so he discovered that just as Galilee had been run by aliens, so too it is outsiders who control the lives of those living in our inner cities today. The rich had prospered from Galilee, but they did not choose to live there. Galilee, as today, produced abundant crops, but the wealth of that produce was rarely consumed by the locals. Indeed, the area was experienced as a no-go area for the elite who garrisoned it with troops when necessary and sent in riot squads when the populace gave vent to their frustrations. All this had made the Galileans renowned for their independence of mind and culture, and the harsh attitude they had to outsiders. Even their accent was readily recognisable outside their own 'turf'. All this and so much more rings numerous bells with the experience of those who live their lives in our inner cities and on our outer housing estates. John Vincent therefore determined to take a social step downwards and follow Jesus in spending his life with the poor. The rest of his life has therefore been lived in that inner-city environment, which seems so readily to resonate with the ethos of the Gospel texts.

Having thus gained this 'hermeneutical advantage' the next stage was to address the text in a way very different from other scholars. For having acknowledged the resonance between Jesus's place and his new place, and having already perceived the instinctive empathy of the people with whom he now lived with the people who surrounded Jesus, he now had a third and vital step to take. And this was where John Vincent took after his namesake, John the Baptist.

For what we all soon learn from inner-city ministry is that belief in 'belief' is a very western, classist matter. People in an inner city or outer housing-estate environment will allow you to believe anything you like, up to a point, but they will be very concerned about what you're going to do about it! They will not be content until you 'put your money where your mouth is.' They know precisely what Jesus meant when he advised his disciples that, "by their fruits you shall know them."

The reason for John the Baptist's attack on the Pharisees was that whilst they appeared totally to accept the mandates of the faith and certainly taught them with a rigour which was convincing, in fact they did not live out the spirit of the Mosaic law in their daily lives. They gave the impression of a liberal openness to the peasantry and yet they used the laws of Sabbath and Jubilee as a means of holding the poor in penury. They were so out of touch with the lives of the poor peasantry that they did not perceive how it was that the loans upon which the poor were dependant could never be paid off if they were not allowed to earn on the Sabbath and if loans would be forfeited in the Jubilee Year. But John the Baptist was at one with the people and could see that the words and the fruits of the Pharisees did not stack up. To the Pharisees the Baptist's prophesies must have come as a horrid surprise - just as John Vincent has never been a welcome prophet today amongst those who are not listening intently to the poor.

Vincent began to see quite clearly that it was not belief constructs that mattered to John the Baptist or indeed to Jesus, as much as one's "Discipleship" - which is committed action within the solidarity of membership of the Movement. Inner city people were indicating to Vincent that the original purpose of the Gospel text was not to impart abstractions but to share accounts of what happens in Jesus's company. The discipleship group is in the company of Jesus sharing what then happens to them when they risk his company. They find out the meaning of the text as things happen in their own experience which resonate with what seems to have been happening with his first disciples. As Vincent says, "Biblical narrative stands as the "midpoint" between the prime Gospel action and the Gospel action today. The biblical text is the interpretative medium between the original action of Jesus and the present action of the Jesus people in the contemporary world." ("Mark's Gospel in the Inner City", p. 286)

It is because of this methodology that the writings of John Vincent therefore take on not only a vibrancy and life but an integrity which even the non-city dweller begins to perceive. The 'praxis' of informing one's action with constant reflection upon the Gospel text, and of interpreting the text by virtue of the Gospel activity in which one is engaged, brings insight to the text. In turn, the new pertinency of the text for their situation, enlivens the poor with both new insight and awareness of the part they have to play in the liberating action of the Gospel in our times.

But to do all this effectively, John Vincent warns that it will be necessary to "Stay in the City" with honesty and integrity, and not to turn the Parables into an elaborate game of Charades. To this end the Urban Theology Unit has been in the forefront in Britain of what we might call 'Social Analysis", which is the determined addressing of the complex issues of our society as experienced from the perspective of the poor and those most hurt by the dynamics of those issues. For it was not for nothing that Jesus spent the first thirty years of his life as a member of his oppressed community. It is only in this way that Jesus can say, "Blessed are the poor," with the integrity which demands attention. If he had made such a claim from the touch-line we might have taken him to be a Pharisee offering a spiritual palliative to the oppressed. But here is 'the Jesus of the Inner City' who has touched base with his people, and whose theology therefore touches the raw nerve of Gospel Good News.

* * * * * * *

But now I want to ask my colleague John Vincent a question. Within the recent decades of our society's history is there growing up yet another group of people who may have a similar 'hermeneutical advantage' with the text? For, alongside the inner city poor, might not a hermeneutical advantage also be experienced by those who, up till now, thought they had it made?

If we take time to re-read the <u>Faith in the City</u> report, there we will find the hope for a society which offers the poor the rewards of the wealth of our society - better housing, health, employment, education and so on. There must be, says our Christian conscience, a better distribution of the good things that our wealthy society has to offer so that all may partake of its opportunities. This seems only right and good, and the report is to be applauded. But is that it? Is that to be the outcome of our discipleship? Is that the New Jerusalem for which Jesus lived and died, and is that therefore to be our Kingdom vision? It is certainly the vision which inspires many of our friends in the inner city who would take the Lottery money tomorrow and run to the suburbs if they ever had the choice. And in this respect I think we would agree that their response does not really resonate with the Gospel text! But on the other hand we can see the sense of 'getting out' because the last thing we want to do from our hermeneutical advantage point is to romanticise the oppression and poverty of the poor alongside whom we have chosen to live.

Most in our present society, and many of those who used to live in our inner cities, have recently been made prisoners to a dream based upon the promise of success and reward. By adopting what is sometimes taken to be the old 'Protestant Work Ethic' it has been assumed that it is possible for all to work out their own salvation. This entails undertaking very demanding personal training and a determination to put off till tomorrow the rewards which will surely come through hard work and self-sacrifice. And many have experienced the truth of the maxim, and through dint of very hard work and self-sacrifice have got out of the inner cities and the depressed housing estates. Some political parties have adopted the same ideology to their own ends and made promises accordingly. "Work hard and you will receive reward and success."

But of late there has arisen in the consciousness of many concerned people a thorough discontent with this dominant myth of our culture. They have worked and aspired and many have attained the rewards which have been on offer. But it has not proved to be the New Jerusalem which was promised. There is a dissatisfaction and uneasiness about the emptiness of the dream. More and more people who have "made it" to the suburbs find themselves exhausted by the rat-race, up to their ears in mortgage debt, terrified about their children's addictions and disillusioned about the probabilities of the future. Maybe I too am prone to romanticise, but I just wonder whether those who have in this way now become despondent with the dominant myths of our society are also in a good place to pick up on the inner meaning of the Gospel texts. After all, many of them, especially those here where I live in Essex, have been born and bred in the slums themselves, so they know the score. They know the pain and the solidarity of suffering, yet they also now know that the promises of worldly wealth (even as espoused in the <u>Faith in the City</u> Report), when once achieved, can still ring surprisingly hollow. And I am not for one moment suggesting that any resonating with the Gospel text which they are able to achieve can be acceptable without resulting action ('by their fruits you will know them' indeed) but it is perhaps possible that they will be in a very good place to understand what John the Baptist is crying out in "the wilderness" - and respond.

There are two personal reasons that bid me ask this question. First, these last four years have proved to be the first in my life during which I no longer live in the inner city, and I have had some surprises. I find that I no longer need to resort to romanticism as an excuse for the horrors of the inner city. Let's not pretend it's pleasant to live in poverty and danger of violence. Jesus would surely want people out of there. And some of those who are out, are wanting to know what they can do to assist in bringing others out of that slavery. But to ask those people who have got out of that physical slavery to return to it, does not seem to help, even if it does offer an hermeneutical advantage in biblical scholarship. If Jesus has nothing to say to those who are not poor any longer except, "get poor again," then surely we're not reading the text right after all. If however he is saying 'Repent', adopt a new mind-set and with this Gospel awareness enter the battle wherever you are in order to see the world change for those around you, then that does make a lot of sense. And who knows, while they may not end up being in a good place to understand the

Gospel of Mark, they may be better placed to make sense for us of the Gospel of John or the Epistles of Paul.

My second reason for asking the question is that deep down I am still convinced by John Vincent's arguments but I want him to tell me what Jesus had that John the Baptist did not. For John the Baptist had a Discipleship group. He too lived out his life in the poverty of Galilee. He too confronted the powers and principalities, and he too had to pay the supreme price. John Vincent, in his book <u>Starting all over Again</u> offers us a radical and new Christology painting pictures of Jesus as Loner, Deviant, Bondman, Juggler, Politician and Pied Piper, but John Vincent doesn't tell us that Jesus was God. And I believe that it's in this area that we will discover the essential difference between what John the Baptist has to offer and what is on offer from Christ.

This is why the story of the incarnation of God in Jesus is so 'telling'. Billions of people have been born in poverty, but never before, to our knowledge, has God. Other people have had disciples and have preferred the simple life style and "journey downwards", but this is God. So with Jesus we are seeing not simply that human beings can do this sort of thing, but we are learning that the Transcendent, the Divine, is in the midst. John Vincent is reluctant to talk too much about these things but it is actually what gets him into all this active theologising in the first place. It is when we see John Vincent expounding his theology and observe the broad, open-eyed grin emerge as he speaks of God's preparedness to share at our vulgar and meagre level, that the essence of John's theology begins to come home to us. It is when we read his Christmas sermons on the incarnation that we begin to sense John Vincent's naive amazement at the audacity of the God who chooses to come as a baby to Bethlehem and hence his amazement at the God who chooses to be in Pitsmoor with Sheffield's poor and forgotten people - to be Jesus in the inner city. ("Christmas on Our Street", 1996)

And if God was in Christ, then the Cross is more than a dreadful mistake which often befalls courageous leaders, not a blip on the canvas of creation, but the very nature of God writ large. And if the cross, then the Resurrection too speaks of more than the fanciful hopes of some first century peasants. And if this is so, then the discipleship group can begin to talk of itself as the Body of Christ. And dare I say, as a sacramentalist Anglican, it is this insight into what it is to "discern the Body" that in the end speaks so powerfully to me in John Vincent's writing.

I was recently listening to a friend of mine who had been walking the Peaks with his family. They had taken a week or so to do it and he explained that, as his body had become more attuned to the physical labour of the demanding walk, so he came to appreciate that his sedentary job had taken from him the joy of what it was to be a bodily creature. We hear it said that an "out of the Body experience" is an extraordinary state, but as he shared his experience with me it began to dawn that for most of us today it is a rarity to be "in the Body". But to "discern the Body" should be, says St Paul, a characteristic state of the Eucharistic community. And it is this incarnational, dare I say sacramental reality that fires John Vincent. John's abiding concern, the discipleship group, is the body that prays, that worships, that listens, analyses and acts out the Gospel happenings. It is not a sedentary abstraction but a Church that puts its bodily money where its thoughtful mouth is.

John Vincent has often been a voice crying in the wilderness of the city but he has always been careful to prepare the way of the Lord.

GOSPEL

From the beginning we have seen how Jesus personally helps those victimised by the system, so that they are able to grab hold of some life for themselves. The lepers, blind, maimed, paralytic and law breakers are restored. Restoration happens in three ways - first to themselves as full persons, second to their families as full members, third to Israel as participant members. And only when Israel refuses to receive them does the counter-community of the Kingdom have to replace the old Israel.

Jesus raises up the social and political weaklings - the poor, the little people, the servants and the children. His disciples still cannot see it. In response to a debate specifically on the nature and persons of power he ridicules 'lording it over others', and demands that first people are servants of all .(Mark, 10. 35-45)

It all becomes clear when Jesus reaches Jerusalem. He enters the great city riding on an ass, 'a colt on which no-one has ridden before' (11.2). And his disciples proclaim 'blessings on the Kingdom of our father David, which is about to come' (11.10). No-one can be confused about the claim. It is a new reality, a new political set-up, a new system of everything that is being announced. And it can only be symbolised by a powerless, untrained, youthful animal, which could not overthrow anyone, except perhaps its rider!

The Kingdom of the powerless, the untrained, the youthful, conflicts hopelessly with the kingdom of the powerful, the sophisticated and the established. Hence, the cleansing of the temple (11.15-18) is designed to cast out the rich and the robbers who made money out of others' needs, and to re-establish the poor, the outsiders, and the Gentiles, for whom it had been intended and who are kept out by the money-changers who demand that Gentile money be changed for Temple money.

In its place, Jesus confirms his own Temple in humanity and his synagogue in the home. He demolishes religion's control over *the after-life (12.18-27), overturns the Davidic supremacy (12.35-37), upholds the selfgiving of the poor above the stewardship of the rich (12.41-44), replaces the Temple (13.1-2), interprets the present and future Israel solely in terms of himself (13.3-37), has his own private anointing outside the Temple (14.3-9), arranges an alternative Passover (14.12-16) and institutes his substitute Passover, the Eucharist (14.17-25).*

Thus Jesus the counter-politician draws up the lines of his alternative politics. First, he sets out his own stall - the ass, the cleansing, the anointing, the last supper. Second, he exposes the existing powers - the Temple, the Romans, the chief priests, the Pharisees, Herodians, Sadducees and scribes. Third, he sets up alternative objects as models - the child, the colt, the little ones, the anointing woman, the widow. Fourth, he sets up a place where these alternative realities can be acted out and supported - the disciple group.

Radical Jesus, 1986, pp 80 - 81

THE JOURNEY DOWNWARDS

CHRIS ROWLAND

After returning from Brazil in 1983, a visit whose effects on my life I am still coming to terms with, I felt the need to seek to relate what I had experienced with my life as a theologian (I was then living and working in Cambridge). I had come across John years before at a student conference when I was an ordinand in Cambridge. All I recall about that meeting was experiencing the righteous indignation and sense of distance between John and myself. I had read material from UTU in the meantime and other friends had contact there. It seemed an obvious thing to do to make contact with those who were doing theology in ways which were kin to what I had witnessed in Brazil. The encounter with John that August afternoon in 1983 was so very different from the one a decade before. It was the beginning of a friendship which has seen me visiting UTU regularly to lecture and share in its work ever since.

That is not to say that there haven't been difficulties. Arising out of that first meeting John and I agreed that I should bring some students from Cambridge to UTU the following spring. Because of my illness that had to be postponed. But in 1985 I brought a dozen or so students to UTU. It was a lively three days. There was lot of argument and some resentment. But what has stayed with me was the heart of the difference between the two groups. John, controversially and provocatively, came up with the typology that students in Cambridge could not be disciples of Jesus but were equipped to be saints. In other words, there was something about living and working in a centre of privilege like Cambridge that militated against a life of discipleship. He was not saying that is was impossible to be a Christian in Cambridge (thought doubtless some heard him to be saying that). What I found remarkable in retrospect was the way in which this corresponded to the kind of sociological typology which undergirded the sociological approaches to early Christianity of Gerd Theissen and Wayne Meeks which were then very much in vogue. In the work of the former a distinction is made between the lifestyle of the wandering charismatics whose outlook is represented in the synoptic tradition and the more settled existence of the first urban Christians of the Pauline mission. Their ethical attitudes were different: a radical lifestyle contrasting with a more staid love patriarchalism which made compromises with the surrounding mores precisely because it was more closely related to it.

Apart from echoing the debates in contemporary New Testament scholarship, that experience at UTU neatly encapsulates a typical feature of John's biblical hermeneutics. When I first started coming, the content of the biblical reflection was devoted almost entirely to Mark. Now I realise that my experience was partial, and that, if I had attended a course for a whole year, many other dimensions of biblical theology might have been on offer, but the ethos of John's discourse was dominated by the Gospel of Mark. It was as if there was a canon within the canon provided by a text which in effect made much of Scripture redundant. The interpretation of this gospel, however, so evident too in many of John's writings, captures the lively challenge of the life of discipleship. Nevertheless other New Testament writings were either criticised or more often neglected in favour of this radical gospel. Two things emerge.

First, the influence of John's study of Mark pervaded UTU in those early years. There was a sense of marginalisation even sectarian isolation over against the rest of the church. Here was a pioneering setting where an option for the poor was being attempted, not by a fleeting acquaintance but by lives lived in the inner city. Every time I go through the Wicker arch en route to Abbeyfield Road, I think back to John's description of it as the dividing line between poor and affluent Sheffield. There was that sense of isolation, of a place which had been forgotten about by the wider church as it got on with its ecclesiastical business, neglectful of the gospel and the poor and needy which it challenges us to serve. I think things are very different now. It is not that the Markan sectarian ethos has gone, but that there is a more ecumenical spirit around. Other bits of the Bible are explored, and there is the recognition that over the last thirty years the tide is beginning to change in the church, in John's direction. He is not a lone voice and his way of doing theology has been influential on the wider Church's training and ministry.

Secondly, John's use of the gospel of Mark fits in with the use of that gospel as a manifesto for a radical political theology in other parts of the world. The emphasis on the politics of discipleship, its cost, the socio-political character of the Galilee/Jerusalem contrast and the priority given to "following" over "thinking" which I have heard in so much of what John has said is encapsulated in books like Radical Jesus and Secular Christ.[1] For John the experience of "the journey downwards" and "the radical alternative" to the religio-political life of his day mirrors his own experience of seeking an alternative space for following and understanding Jesus Christ. "Re-education" through "relocation" is what John and the Urban Theology Unit have offered over the years and John finds this in that alternative learning space set up by Jesus, according to Mark's gospel, in the house or intimate meals rather than synagogue or Temple.

It is not always recognised how much John anticipated trends in Markan scholarship and liberation hermeneutics. I want to examine two examples of the exegesis of Mark which exhibit this particular approach.

Fernando Belo [2] (followed by Michel Clevenot[3]) has used contemporary literary criticism as well as Marxism in search of an analysis of the text of Mark as a social product. He analyses the text to lay bare the social conflicts. The text is viewed as the juxtaposition of different types of textual material (myth, parable, discourse, narrative) playing different functions within the narrative. Belo suggests that there are two distinct systems represented in the Torah, one based on Leviticus (what he calls the pollution system) and one based on Deuteronomy (the debt system which is specifically concerned with social equality), indicative of previous conflicts within Judaism. The Levitical system, centred as it is on the cult and the privileges of the priests, contrasts with the Deuteronomic system which promoted social justice and cohesion rather than division based on caste and ritual purity. According to Belo the priestly caste was responsible for the final form of the canon and thus gave their class power a solid foundation in the ideological deposit. It is with the radicalised version of the system based on Deuteronomy that Belo considers that Jesus sides over against the system promoted by the cult, the Temple in Jerusalem, the economic power base of a priestly and aristocratic elite in Jerusalem.

Jesus is presented as one who subverts the prevailing ideological consensus, particularly the system based on Leviticus. In the early part of the gospel there is gradually articulated a division between Jesus and the disciples on the one hand and the crowds on the other. Jesus' strategy is to avoid the towns, centres of the crowds and the authorities, and when he cannot escape, to create a space for himself and his disciples as they learn a different, counter-cultural life. Belo repeats the opinion of many scholars that Jesus was not a Zealot, whose goal, he claims, was not revolution which would completely abolish the existing economic order, but a rebellion which would restore it to its pristine form. Belo argues that Jesus came to Jerusalem to preach in the Temple to proclaim that in the light of the rejection that was taking place, the "vineyard" (Mk. 12.1ff) would be given to others and then himself to move on to the wider world. There was only one way in which Jesus' non-violent communism could have been extended in a situation where the Roman economic and political system was so powerful, other than by marginalisation like the Essenes, and that was by means of opening up the gospel to the nations. It is the transfer of Judas from the circle of disciples to the circle of the dominant class as an informant that enables the hierarchy to put an end to Jesus' strategy, which is thereby interrupted incomplete. Just before he dies, however, he predicts his imminent death and gets the disciples to focus themselves on shared bread rather than his own person as a symbol of continued commitment of his mission. In the course of his career Jesus challenges the current conceptions of the family, the centrality of the Temple and the hegemony of the priests' wealth, and rejects the conventional master/servant relationship. For Belo, Jesus' message is "non-violent communism".

A major feature of Belo's interpretation is his view that we have in Mark the juxtaposition of a narrative, centred on the miracles and the radical teaching, and a more theological (or ideological in Marx's sense) discourse which permeates the second half of the gospel and offers an explanation of Jesus' death. Belo suggests that these theological ideas about cross and the necessity of suffering have begun to disguise the central importance of the narrative of Jesus' radical praxis. The task of a liberationist exegesis is to restore the priority of that praxis for Jesus, from a text where it has begun to be subordinated to theological reflection at the expense of the political character of Jesus' life and death.

Belo's reading of Mark exposes the way in which the text of Mark is itself a combination of a story of radical change in the first part of the gospel, interrupted by an emerging preoccupation with theological reflection on the significance of Jesus' death. In Mark the story of the execution of a subversive messianic claimant is thus on the way to becoming an otherworldly myth which involves an escape from issues of justice. Jesus' bloody execution by the Romans as a martyr for the kingdom is uprooted from its historical context and made into a timeless abstraction. The interruption of the subversive story of Jesus is a reflection of the political powerlessness of the first Christians who found no adequate outlet for their messianic enthusiasm. The political structures offered little space for change. Telling the story of Jesus in this form reflects the frustration of those who seek to live in the way of the Messiah amidst a hostile environment.

Writing in the wake of Belo's work, Ched Myers in his book on Mark writes an extended commentary[4]. Myers holds no formal academic position but is active in Quaker justice and peace issues in the USA. In it he maps the social world of Mark and its readers, paying particular attention to the interest in countryside and ordinary people over against the economic interests of the metropolis. Evidence of popular protest as means of expressing discontent is in Josephus' writings (War i.650; Antiquities 55 and 267). Myers' thesis is that Mark's gospel comes from a group that is alienated from the dominant order yet is still politically engaged. The setting of the gospel in the last years of the Jewish revolt is the context for the challenge to the community to reject violent revolution in favour of a non-violent attempt to set up an alternative society. The community differed from those like the Jewish freedom fighters (loosely termed Zealots) who wanted to reform the existing order. There is challenge to the centrality of Jerusalem, Davidic messianism and the boundaries of the purity code. Myers describes one of Mark's major themes as a "war of myths" between a dominant ideology and an emerging counter-culture based on Jesus and his practice. Drawing on the language of the Apocalypse he sees a "two level" struggle going on in which Jesus is engaged with the powers opposed to God whether heavenly or earthly.

Myers reads the gospel as a sophisticated narrative form of the "Christus Victor" theology in which the economic, institutional and spiritual power of the Temple is destroyed at the moment of Jesus' death to be replaced by a "counter-culture" based on service. Conventional ties are loosed and custom is abandoned for a new way (1.40; 2.23ff; 5.25; 7.10). This "good news" contrasts with the secular "evangel" of the imperial propaganda and challenges that dominant ideology. Mark's Jesus challenges a culture of status and customary practice and institutions. In 10.42 the disciples want to sit and rule but are only offered baptism and a cup of suffering. There is to be an alternative perspective in the circle of disciples, learning to be free of dominant ways of looking at the world (4.18; 8.28ff), and characterised by the taking up a cross (8.34ff; 10.42ff), a rebel's fate.

The gospel is not merely about the propounding of an alternative but also predicts the destruction of the present religio-political order which is intimately linked with the death of Jesus. Within the context of the gospel as a whole Jesus' death comes at the end of a narrative in which from Ch.11 onwards a dominant theme is the Temple. Jesus is portrayed as a prophet of doom teaching in the centre of the Jewish empire and attracting a mixed response. The Temple is not only of narrowly religious significance, in Myers commentary, for it is seen as at the heart of a socio-economic complex of great importance for most Jews. From the moment that Jesus enters the Temple it is apparent from Mark that the cursing of the fig tree which sandwiches the so-called "Cleansing of the Temple" comments thereby on the bankruptcy of that institution, suggesting that its fate will be that of the cursed tree. But elsewhere in 13.28 the fig tree is used as a sign of imminent change. The destruction of the Temple may also be the moment of the growth of something new in the "counter-culture" proposed by Jesus.[5]

While the commentary is full of suggestive ideas, as a genre it stands closer to mainstream biblical scholarship than the commentaries on Mark such as those of Fernando Belo and Michel Clevenot. The historical approach to the text is juxtaposed with a close reading which owes much to narrative criticism, so that at the end of the day doubts about the particular historical reconstruction need not detract from the value of the insights into the plot and themes of the text. In many ways it is rooted in the mainstream of a modern biblical scholarship which is struggling to maintain faithfulness to its historical critical past, while exploring, perhaps rather late in the day, other literary approaches as well as the socio-political dimension of all reading.

Approaches like these have met with either a muted response or complete indifference from mainstream biblical scholarship. Neither Belo's nor Myer's work commands much attention. This has been the case with liberationist hermeneutics generally. There may be sympathy for the predicament and commitment of the practitioners but the results of the exegesis are not seen as a real contribution to exegetical debate. So when constructive comment and criticism comes it is to be welcomed.

One of the most significant has been from the Pontifical Biblical Commission[6]. In a review of methods of biblical interpretation it considers liberation theology. The report indicates that it adopts no particular methodology but "starting from its own socio-cultural and political point of view, it practices the reading of the bible which is oriented to the needs of the people. From this will come authentic Christian praxis leading to the transformation of society". It regrets too great a concentration on narrative and prophetic texts which highlight situations of oppression and which inspire a praxis leading to social change, and warns, in words which John, I am sure would want strenuously to oppose, that "while it is true that exegesis cannot be neutral, social and political action is not the direct task of the exegete". There is a suspicion of a Marxist agenda. "Some theologians and exegetes have made use of various instruments for the analysis of social reality ... and have conducted an analysis inspired by materialist doctrines. It is within such a frame of reference that they have also read the bible, a practice which is very questionable, especially when it involves the Marxist principle of class struggle." Also, there is a recognition that "understandably, there has been more emphasis on an earthly eschatology ... to the detriment of the more transcendent dimensions of scriptural eschatology."

In addition to its rather mild comments on liberation theology there is a much more trenchant criticism of Feminist Exegesis which led to a clear difference of opinion in the Commission.

".. to the extent that Feminist Exegesis proceeds from a preconceived judgement. it runs the risk of interpreting the biblical texts in a tendentious and thus debatable manner. To establish its positions it must often for want of something better have recourse to arguments *e silentio* ... The attempt made on the basis of fleeting indications in the texts to reconstitute a historical situation which these same texts are considered to have been designed to hide does not correspond to the work of exegesis properly so called. It entails rejecting the content of the inspired texts in preference for a hypothetical reconstruction, quite different in nature."

"Feminist exegetes need to beware that they ... not lose sight of the evangelical teaching concerning power and service, a teaching addressed by Jesus to all disciples, men and women."

Let me make some comments on all of this. Firstly, there are echoes of the criticism of the first, harsher critique of liberation theology in the Commission's criticism of the use of Marxist analysis. Although the influence of Norman Gottwald on popular education material on the Old Testament in Latin America is widespread, particularly the popular revolt theory of the Exodus, Marxist, or any other principle of class struggle, hardly influences liberation exegesis otherwise. Secondly, the emphasis on earthly eschatology is quite correct and it follows a stream of theology which is widespread in our century (Jurgen Moltmann might be cited as a European exponent of it). The Commission's assumption that scriptural eschatology is more transcendent reflects one side of a hotly contested debate about early Christian eschatology. Liberation theology has opened our eyes to alternative approaches to eschatology, different from the Augustinian consensus, in early and later Christian tradition.

The criticism of feminist theology strikes a rather discordant note in such a balanced report. Whose exegesis, we may ask, is *not* in danger of "proceeding from a preconceived judgement, and running the risk of interpreting the biblical texts in a tendentious and debatable manner"? This seems to me to be an apt description of the historical-critical method, the method which the commission regards as "indispensable", because it operates with the help of scientific criteria that seek to be as objective as possible. But the process of reconstruction and hypothesis as a key determinant of a text's meaning is the bread and butter of the historical-critical method. Textual "archaeology" achieves the digging underneath the literary remains to reconstruct the life of particular Christian communities, another story which functions as a determining commentary on the literal sense of the text. So a gospel narrative becomes (as it were) a window onto the life of the church. Characters in the narrative can become ciphers for different groups seeking to expound or reject the

Christian legacy. I think that one might justifiably argue that this approach is a modern form of spiritualising or allegorical exegesis, though of course, unlike patristic application of the method, the referent to the hidden story is history rather than the higher truths of divinity.

There is, it seems to me, a naivete about the view of the historical-critical method on the part of the Commission. In particular, the view that scholars who practise it, "have ceased combining this method with a philosophical system" and are so now free of the "preconceived judgements" of other methods. (Is this an example of the exponents of a dominant ideology thinking that what they do is normal or common sense?) In the report the liberationist and feminist interpretations are both given the label "contextual approaches" as if the historical-critical methods is not contextual. In its assessment of the liberationist perspectives its sympathetic tone yet contrasts with the lukewarm reaction to it by the most "Northern" exegetes.

The liberal exegetes have been ambivalent in their reaction. Typical is that of Leslie Houlden who considered it in a short editorial in Theology in 1990 and sounded a gently sceptical note[7]. Houlden welcomed their work, but thought that they were not served well by what he called their "Northern imitators". He mounted a defence of conventional biblical study using the historical method as practised in most departments of theology. To Houlden, liberation exegesis seemed to be harking back to the banished voice of yesteryear in its apparent concern to promote a new form of biblical theology. The exegesis of the base ecclesial communities seems to him "little more than the discernment of scriptural analogies to present situations and concerns" which "is essentially the procedure of every devout Bible study group in Christendom". He wondered whether the liberation theologians have capitulated too much to the spirit of the age and expressed the view that "the Bible has other jobs to do than dance to our late twentieth century favourite tunes."

In believing that we have much to learn from liberationist exegesis I do not want to assert that everything about is to be slavishly followed. There are elements of it that I find problematic: for example, the reliance on historical reconstruction, whether it be the origins of Israel or the historical Jesus. But for all that I think Barth is a herald of the sentiments of many liberation theologians when he said in his preface to Romans, "Why should parallels drawn from the ancient world be of more value for our understanding of the epistle than the situation in which we ourselves actually are and to which we can therefore bear witness?"[8] Despite the impression that they "make the Bible dance to twentieth century tunes" I think that a liberation exegesis has in common with the mainstream biblical study a concern to be critical. Indeed, "Northern" exegesis can thank the liberationist perspective for the incessant reminder of its own partiality, as the Commission document reminds us. In particular, we need to be reminded that "drawing from the text simply what it contains" (to quote Leslie Houlden's words) ignores the complex process which is involved in giving meaning to texts. Successful exegesis requires eisegesis in order to extract whatever it may contain.

John and I have been involved from the very start with the British Liberation Theology Consultation. To it come people engaged in biblical study which resembles that criticised by Leslie Houlden. What is apparent to me is that there is a growing gap between the use of the bible in adult theological education in Britain, and its use in theology and religious studies departments and most seminaries. That was brought home to me when I attended the conference of ACATE two years ago for the first time. The Association of Centres of Adult Theological Education includes a variety of people in very different contexts engaged in theological education with adults: continuing ministerial trainers; adult education officers in the churches; tutors on non-residential ministerial courses and many others. The ethos of pedagogy there was experiential and was similar to that promoted by John. I consider it part of my task as a theologian in higher education to try and forge links between the biblical studies which predominates in a university like Oxford and what I hear and learn from the practitioners at the British Liberation Theology Consultations. Frequenty there is an understanding of the scriptures which has passed me by in my context. I sense that there is a risk of a polarisation as the two streams go their own ways. The Latin American experience and John's work suggests that it need not be so. There is a way that they can be held together and indeed benefit one another. Modern biblical study is a hermeneutical maelstrom, and it would be a pity if British exegesis did not allow itself to be influenced by currents of interpretation which are fructifying both church and academy in other parts of the world, and are outside the ambit of the theological departments and seminaries.

What John has steadfastly borne witness to has its parallels in exegesis and pedagogy in this country and in other parts of the world. I am sure he still feels that he and UTU are marginal to theology and church. In a way he is right. I guess that still for many people mention of John and UTU can function like the red rag to the ecclesiastical and theological bulls. I have on several occasions found myself saying to John that in several important respects he has won the argument. UTU may not be the centre of the theological universe (though its growing links with the department of Biblical Studies in Sheffield is an indication of the forward-looking attitude of that department and John's recognition of the importance of some institutional support). Nevertheless the "Vincentian hermeneutical circle"[9] which John was pioneering long before liberation and contextual theology became all the rage is firmly entrenched in theological courses up and down Britain. In this John's role, day in and day out hammering away, sometime seemingly repetitively so, about an option for the inner city and the role of context in theology, has been indispensable in transforming theological education in these islands. His written work and that of supporters at UTU lacks the polish and sophistication to be taken seriously as theology. Like his favourite New Testament book, the gospel of Mark, it is not part of the work of the literary or educational elite and is geared to provide stimulus and wisdom arising from and for those at the grassroots, unbuttressed by footnotes or extensive bibliographies. Consequently few will take notice of it, nor can it form a central part of publishers' catalogues. In a sense it is not marketable because it does not nearly conform to what is expected of theology. But theology it is, challenging the hegemony of those who presume to know what theology is and excluding that which does not conform to its canons. Doubtless John could, as he has often said, gone down another path and ended up as a distinguished lecturer or professor in a department of theology. But his genius has been to go down that other route, not turning his back on the academy but forming an academy in the inner-city which articulates wisdom from the conventional academy's books and offers space for it to mix with the insights of people with little or no formal education who have sensed the called of God and the wisdom of Christ in ways hidden from the wise of this world. And I thank God for that and for John's role in it.

1 J Vincent, Radical Jesus (1986) and Secular Christ (1968)
2 F Belo A Materialist Reading of the Gospel of Mark, New York 1981, discussed by C Rowland in New Blackfriars 65 (1984) pp. 157ff.
3 M Clevenot Materialist Approaches to the Bible New York 1985
4 C Myers Binding the Strong Man New York 1988. There is a version for use by study groups with an overtly contemporary agenda in Myers, Say to this Mountain New York 1997

5 Note the similar line but from the perspective of historical criticism in K Wengst, Pax Romana and the Peace of Jesus Christ London 1988
6 Leslie Houlden The Interpretation of the Bible in the Church (1995)
7 Leslie Houlden "Schools of Thought" Theology 93 (1990)
8 K Barth The Epistle to the Romans
9 A diagrammatic presentation awawiting publication

STORY-MAKING

Theology takes place as the people of God see themselves as part of the biblical story, project themselves into that story and then project that story out into their corporate and individual lives. It arises from Disciples of Jesus Christ looking in a mirror to discern who they are as Christians.

All theology is a variety of paradigms with which one interacts and reflects as a Christian while part of the gospel unfolds. It is the end point in a process - a personal discipline, arising from a particular person at a particular time and in a particular time and in a particular context seeking to address a particular issue of the church, the world or the Christian life.

"Remnant Theology as the Base for Urban Ministry", 1995, p. 25

You must change from being a story-reader into being a story-maker.

Mark at Work, 1986, p.18

****

TOWARDS AN URBAN HERMENEUTICS

ANDREW DAVEY

Those of us who have worked with John Vincent over the years will have heard a consistent call to identify and exploit biblical and historical paradigms as part of the process of discernment in our own discipleship. "Ask yourselves," students on various study programmes will have been challenged, "where have people like me, in a community like mine, been faced with a situation like mine, entered into a struggle and proved faithful?"

If one is allowed to impose a paradigm on someone else, it is the seventeenth century prophets who come to mind when one thinks about a certain twentieth century prophet who looks for the actualisation of the gospel community as a counter challenge within contemporary church and society. In his account of the role of the Bible in the seventeenth century revolution Christopher Hill recalls the words of the Welsh pamphleteer Arise Evans:

> I looked upon the Scripture as a history of things that passed in other countries, pertaining to other people; but now I looked upon it as a mystery to be opened at this time belonging to us all. [1]

The digger leader Gerrard Winstanley claimed that scripture was being "really and materially fulfilled" [2] in the St George's Hill commune, the very existence of which challenged the interests of Fairfax and the other commonwealth leaders.

Many of those working in the urban scene in Britain and elsewhere have been inspired to interact with the scriptures in a way that defies the traditional exegetical methods received through theological education. It was work from the two-thirds world that often gave hints about the possibility of a new hermeneutics "from below". Insights from Cardenal's Solentiname Community in Nicaragua or Charles Avila's *Peasant Theology* in the Philippines provided encouragement that such a community reading could happen. At a basic level hermeneutics has been defined as interpretation. Those who have taken part in theology and Bible workshops at UTU have been encouraged over the years to discover "the hermeneutics of suspicion" and "hermeneutic cycle" of the liberation theologians for themselves, to identify paradigms and establish new readings which utilise the insights of contemporary biblical scholarship - but more importantly use the context of the reader as the raw material which the encounter with scripture will begin to reshape. It was this that caught the attention of (now Bishop) Barbara Harris in the mid seventies:

> (UTU's) subscribers make no pretence at being what they are not. They are not, for the most part, economically disadvantaged; with few exceptions, they are not members of ethnic minority groups; nor are they disenfranchised members of the society. They are what they are, but by virtue of their location and focus, they are able to hear things in new ways. They attempt to discern how people hear the story where they

are, and how the gospel story relates to people where they are now. [3]

While encouraging others to put their stories alongside the Biblical text, be they ministers on the DMin or MMin course, peace activists and ecological warriors on the study year, enquirers on various weekends and consultations, John has himself outlined an autobiographical hermeneutics of various projects in urban discipleship, focussed in SICEM and the pioneering members of its congregations.

In 1967 John saw the future of the church in terms of "prophetic deeds ... acted parables ... [and] ... new embodiments" [4]. Ten years later in *Stirrings* he called for a rediscovery of testimony so that new stories might be heard and told:

> All this adds up to a new regard for testimony. What Christians can be heard doing with their stories is significant. What they do with them might be (1) to act in the light of them, (2) to worship or act communally in the light of them, and (3) to tell stories or give witnesses and testimonies about the way the truths contained in them actually "work" for them. [5]

The embodiment of the narrative unleashes and energises the groups involved into new acts and new history. The story of the first twelve years of SICEM as retold in Into the City fuses the narrative of an individual in community, identifying with the gospel story and discerning new ways of realising discipleship. In 1991 John explored some of the processes and questions behind this:

> I want to know not simply what places in the gospel can help me with my place and vocation in the city, but even more, what disciplines and vocations, practice and spirituality, I now as an inner city person need to be open to, in order that the gospel may happen around me; that is, in order that I can also fulfil my vocation as a New Testament student and as a theologian, in my vocation, in the inner city. [6]

John is in good company. Walter Brueggemann understands telling stories to be a vital activity in the community of faith:

> The stories do not exist by themselves nor for themselves. They exist as they are told and valued, transmitted and

remembered by a community which is seriously engaged in a life of ministry and faith. [7]

The Communities which grapple with the scriptures are described variously as "interpretative communities", "receiving communities" and "listening communities". This grappling should lead those communities to define themselves through their communal and individual decisions and actions, that is their ethics. Alan Dale in his retelling of the Old Testament stories - The Winding Quest [8] - places the patriarchal stories amidst the later prophetic writings - the section is titled - "Enduring Convictions". The stories come under the question "What kind of person should we be?" It is interesting to note that the philosopher Alastair MacIntyre sees narrative as a vital element in moral discourse:

> ... man (sic) is in his actions and practice, as well as in his fictions, essentially a story-telling animal. He is not essentially, but becomes through his history, a teller of stories that aspire to truth. But the key question for men is not about their own authorship; I can only answer the question "What am I to do?" if I can answer the prior question "Of what story do I find myself part?" [9]

John had begun this process in Stirrings, where (in the language of the times) he stated "The only unique thing about a man is his own history". [10]

Location is vital to an understanding of John's hermeneutics. The place is the arena of the story. Social location might be considered a fact of life [11] - the totality of the influences, pressures, experiences that shape the lives of individuals and communities, with direct bearing on the interpretation reached. But social location needs to be made explicit. How does our situation affect the way we approach the text? What pressures are we under from others to read as if things were otherwise? What dominant readings need to be rejected because we know the world to be different? How will our encounter with scripture affect the way we understand our situation? Once a Christian disciple brings their place into their reading of the scriptures, a whole new set of possibilities is unleashed.

> ... it becomes a matter of evangelistic common sense or hermeneutic appropriateness that we in biblical studies work as

much with the contemporary contexts of people as we do with the biblical contexts of writers and audiences. [12]

Once one has "found one's place" as location, then one "finds one's place" in the text. And once one has found one's place in the text, then the text comes back and illuminates the location. [13]

Context is where the encounter will take place, from where we will be challenged, and from where connections need to be made with those who are seeking new possibilities. The social location will also include the community in which the reading takes place. That is the possibility which I believe we begin to glimpse as urban communities handle the Bible in new ways. When the community of disciples has real access to the scriptures, transformation, learning through and for liberation, is possible.

The poor in the poor churches suddenly hear things they know from their own experience, reflected back at them in the biblical stories. They discover that according to the Bible, God is on their side. [14]

The Hispanic theologian Eldin Vallafane identifies the rediscovery of the hermeneutical advantage of the poor in the urban church to be a sign of the breaking in of the "Koinonia (or partnership) of the Spirit". [15] Allowing theology to emerge from congregations of marginalised urban people is something that even John admits has barely started. Unleashing that potential is a risk which most churches have not been willing to take or have been blinkered of the need for. [16]

It could mean a new version of the Gospel, from the bottom, from the urban, which would build an urban theology - which would be a new way for us all of learning from as well as learning with the inner city. [17]

The foretaste of that theology is found in much of John's work. In the words of Nicholas Lash: "the fundamental form of Christian interpretation of scripture is the life activity and organisation of the believing community."[18] To facilitate new and diverse retellings through the lives of small Christian communities is part of the vocation of the urban theologian, allowing confidence to develop, enabling people to recognise and name God's reign in their own lives and in the communities of which they are part. That process needs to allow the space for the questioning, the tentative first steps, the imagining of possible futures, the unpredictability and self-expression which many urban communities have been denied, as the stories of faithfulness and resilience emerge which move the protagonists from being readers and listeners to being story-makers.

---

1 Christopher Hill, The English Bible and the Seventeenth Century Revolution, (Allen Lane/Penguin 193), p.40
2 Paul M Siegal, The Meek and the Militant, (Zed Press 1986), p. 94
3 Barbara Harris, "A New Model Training Centre" in Doing Theology in the City 1977
4 JV Here I Stand, p. 64
5 JV Stirrings, p 111
6 JV "Mark's Gospel in the Inner City" 1991 in The Bible and the Politics of Exegesis p. 277
7 Walter Brueggemann, Genesis - A Bible Commentary for Preaching and Teaching, (John Knox 1982) p.4
8 Alan T Dale, Winding Quest - The Heart of the Old Testament in Plain English, (OUP 1972)
9 Alastair MacIntyre, After Virtue, 2nd ed. (Duckworth 1985), p. 216
10 JV Stirrings, p.111
11 See Teresa Okure, "Reading from This Place; Some Problems and Perspectives" in Segovia, Fernando F & Tolbert, Mary Ann, eds., Reading from this Place - Volume 2: Social Location and Biblical Interpretation in Global Perspective, (Fortress Press 1995)
12 JV The Bible and the Politics of Exegesis, p. 281
13 JV The Bible and the Politics of Exegesis, p. 284
14 JV Liberation Theology from the Inner City, p. 8
15 Eldin Villafane, Seek the Peace of the City - Reflections on Urban Ministry, (Eerdmans 1995) p. 29-39
16 See Living Faith in the City (General Synod 1991) 2.14, p. 14
17 JV "An Inner City Learning Community", 1997, p. 12
18 Nicholas Lash, Theology on the Road to Emmaus (SCM 1986) p.43

DYNAMICS

Thus, every Jesus story begins with incarnation - getting where people are, living with them, sharing their lot. It goes on to healing ministry - listening to what people's real needs are, being the patient washer of feet or cleaner of streets or brewer of tea. It then with love and care, not breaking the bruised reed, will seek to lift out into the light the points, people, groups, happenings, which bring love, healing, acceptance, or significance: the ministry of parables. Then perhaps there will be specific actions: not great actions, but small, meaningful, planned, strategic actions which are acted parables, prophetic signs, imaginative instances, which can liberate old elements in the situation , and hold up new possibilities. But all this will throw up and confirm the disciple group; it will force them together, and necessitate a discipline and a corporate mutual reliance. And perhaps there will be 'polarisation', conflict, the parting of the ways, new alliances with strange bedfellows: the cross. And the cross is also the loneliness of the vicarious initiator, who 'does his thing' because it is 'everybody's'. Then, finally, there might be signs of resurrection, as the deed catches on, or the new style evokes response, or the group is thrilled with a momentary success, or the disciple experiences 'the joy of the resurrection'. And occasionally, within the battles of history, we see the parousia, the ultimate triumph of the Way.

The Jesus Thing, 1973, p.60

GOSPEL PATTERNS

ROBIN PAGAN

Introduction

In this paper we shall be considering three of John's books which give us clues into his understanding of the gospel patterns which can help us shape our discipleship and the dynamic which empowers and holds that discipleship together. Two of the books are relatively early efforts to clarify this schema, the first being Secular Christ written in the late '60's and The Jesus Thing from the early '70's. (It should be noted both these books come before that indefinable date where the masculine form of the third person singular was still considered inclusive and quotations from these books will inevitably be uncomfortable to contemporary sensibilities). The Third is the later autobiographical work of the early '80's Into The City which, given his commitment to action, appropriately reflects upon how John's ministry at Sheffield ,and before, has been shaped by these gospel patterns and motivated by what he calls the dynamics of Christ.

This is not to say that we couldn't have used other examples of John's work, as his involvement with these gospel patterns can be noted in several other of his books such as, Radical Jesus (1986) which he finds in Mark's gospel and Starting All Over Again (1981) in which the writer claims, "Christianity is starting all over again." and that "...hints of Jesus in the city remind us of the experiences of the first disciples, and there is much we can learn from them." (cover note). In fact we could say the title of this book, Starting All Over Again tells us something significant about John's approach to the "mystery of Jesus" (SC pp 32-33,190-191). There is a sense in which having found himself persuaded by the patterns and dynamics of the gospel narrative, John has found himself compelled to attempt their clarification over and over again, so that many of his books give the impression of, "starting all over again". In each case , however, there are new insights and facets of the central Jesus mystery revealed, and these inevitably provisional attempts, make fascinating if at times tantalisingly ambiguous reading, as John weaves his variations on his central themes.

These themes or patterns, which will provide us with the substance of this paper, are summarised in John's own words in The Jesus Thing. There, he lists not just the patterns themselves (or at least one version of them, for even these central criteria are up for grabs given John's empirical experimental approach to the subject), but reminds us of their essentially sequential, dynamic nature (see quotation above).

Incarnation

"Far too often the total work of Christ is ignored and the cross and resurrection alone cited as the starting point of the church's existence and action." (S.C. 220f). John insists , however, that the true starting point must be incarnation, hence his emphasis on a Secular Jesus, revealed to us in Mark's gospel;

> "(Mark's) whole story is about Jesus walking, talking, getting into boats, doing controversial things, healing, getting into arguments, evading opponents, securing friends, explaining himself, explaining his teaching. His whole story is a secular event..." (SC p79)

Elsewhere we read, "Jesus was no 'pale Galilean', no figure of sanctity,...Jesus was a working man who'd have given anything for an electric drill and a lathe..." (SC p69). We have, then, an insistence on Jesus' human condition as the basic gospel pattern for the church to take on board if it is not going to hopelessly misunderstand the essential nature of the "Jesus-Event".

"Who you are is where you are" (TJT p37) becomes the gadfly slogan for true incarnation. Of course we know that life cannot accurately be reduced to such formulae but this aphoristic saying retains sufficient truth to give our largely middle class churches an uncomfortable tweak. The church must recognise that;

> "the basic theology of Jesus is an attempt to say that God is where Jesus is, and that Jesus is what he is doing in the place where he stands alongside men." (TJT p38)

Nor is the process of incarnation a comfortable thing to be caught up in, involving as it does a built in option towards the marginalised. John is quite open about his experience;

> "I knew, when I first arrived in inner-city Sheffield, that if I stayed one year, I would have to stay ten...Once the first weeks were through, I could feel myself becoming tied down, and though I hated it for the first few years, now, looking back, I do not see there could have been any other way for things to have grown as they have, if I had rejected that first incarnation into cold, unwelcoming Pitsmoor, and run away from it." (ITC p15).

Healing Ministry

But incarnation in itself is not so extraordinary, we all must be located somewhere. The Christ dynamic, however, requires us to locate in situations of need and that particularly require a healing ministry.

John refers to a "ministry of identification", which "means seeking out the poor, the disinherited, the victims, the handicapped, the disadvantaged,....." (TJT p45), what we have more commonly come to refer to as "God's preferential option for the poor".

In opposition to so much of western religiosity which presents schemes for individuals to 'save their life', comes the call of Jesus to 'lose life for my sake', and for the Good News' sake." (TJT p41)

Again the concept of vocation needs to be put to the test of the same gospel dynamic;

"The conscious and intentional disciple, however, seeks the place and work which crucially need to be done, which impinge most upon his conscience, which are the places most ignored by others, and most like to Jesus's work amongst the forgotten, the outcast, the rejected, the disadvantaged, the incurably sick, the alien." (TJT p43)

If the nature of the proper gospel pattern response is clear enough the appeal to conscience begs the question concerning motivation behind it and what it is that triggers the Christ dynamic within us. On the subject of the nature of this Christ dynamic which moves the gospel process along John writes;

"In the Synoptic Gospels...<u>dynamis</u> is always the dynamic action which healing is. It is neither a 'stuff' that Jesus holds as a settled possession, nor is it a 'power of God from outside' which suddenly descends then disappears, It is the best word the New Testament can find to describe the action of God in Jesus <u>at the moment of its occurrence</u>." (SC p183)

In human terms we might think of it more concretely in terms of the faculty of compassion which is moved to further compassion by witnessing it originally, a sort of chain reaction of compassion.

Where words can only hint at the underlying truth, stories from experience can give us the realities. One such healing story involved one of the struggling inner-city churches John was involved with;

"No one ever went down there and sat with them for a few years and said, `Alright, what have you got going here? How can we protect it and let it grow? How can we forget our institutional demands and expectations, and start working from what you actually have?" (ITC p32)

That the wider "institutional" church has in some cases learned to do something like this is encouraging. But the challenge to many such projects still lies in those incarnational words "for a few years"! Healing takes time and patience.

Parables

The nature of the parables, their purpose and structure continues to be a subject of debate. Andrew Parker is a regular lecturer at UTU and his book, Painfully Clear (Sheffield Academic Press, 1996) is a good example of this. A clue to John's angle is in the sub title to the chapter on parables in Secular Christ, "The hiddenness of the Kingdom". After all, John argues, "Would Jesus have been at all concerned to make the kind of banal moralisms which frequent interpretations of the parables attribute to him?" (SC p111).

But, as Ed Kessler and Andrew Parker have made clear there is no real conflict between clarity and profundity in the parables. Parker's book title reminds us that the parables were "painful", challenging, precisely because they were "clear", understood by their original hearers.

John's emphasis on the "hiddenness" of the Kingdom remains significant, however, if we are to avoid the tendency for us to impose our own agendas onto those of God;

> "...The secular Christ exists in his own right and not merely because modern man thinks he seeks him..." - "a Christ after his own image." (SC p123)

So in his later book John reiterates the hiddenness of the Kingdom within the parable stories and encourages an open discipleship towards them;

> "The disciple oscillates between awaiting, recognising and hailing the signs, yet realising that he cannot recognise the Hidden kingdom... The disciple therefore operates not simply with 'the world as the agenda', but with a hidden agenda also - an agenda of secret understanding, expectation and intention." (TJT p45)

Acted Parables

The lack of any contemporary spoken parables would seem to indicate the disuse of this central "evangelistic strategy" of Jesus. Why might this be? Parables in our day seem unnecessarily obscure and even pompous (e.g. Cantona's effort with the media concerning boats, seagulls and sardines!). A possible reason for this could be that in an open society it is easier and more effective simply to say things straight out , even if they are controversial. In Jesus' day the social and political climate were much more oppressive. Then again it may in part be to do with oratorical style and preferences, and one has to admit that coining spoken parables on the hoof is no easy matter.

In the world of wider political and social action it would appear we have more in common with the world of Jesus. Despite our democratic society, decision makers and centres of power often seem remote and unapproachable. In such circumstances the acted parable comes into its own. What's more, acted parables are events that can be photographed and used evangelically to provide the front cover of a book! (see ITC)

"For me," John writes "the Christian way is above all the way of the acted parable or prophetic sign...First it is meant to tell people what is really going on. Secondly, it is meant to give people the chance to change, to see a new way and to take it. Thirdly, it is meant to expose false commitment and show the true and false as irreconcilables." (ITC 53f)

Elsewhere John speaks somewhat plaintively of "tricking" people into Kingdom action through acted parables ;

"And if only the world - and the disciples - would be content thus to be 'tricked' into being released, through this technique of acting as if things were different, then the dynamic of mutual reconciliation would also be let loose." (TJT p48)

Disciple Group

In Secular Christ John outlines four characteristics of discipleship; (a) being with Jesus, (b) carrying out his healing ministry, (c) fulfilling Christ's way, (d) suffering at the hands of the world." (SC 137ff). In short, discipleship is participation in the gospel patterns and Christ dynamic that we are seeking to describe.

Within this drama the act of following and the acceptance of discipleship are crucial to the ongoing dynamic of the Kingdom and there is little room, if any, for compromise in this demanding vocation;

"The church is thus not constituted by those who 'believe the gospel' but those who 'act out the good news'". "The church does not exist where 'the gospel is faithfully proclaimed and the sacraments duly administered' but where the Jesus-centred life... is continued." (TJT p50)

John has a particular confidence in the small disciple group:

"Everywhere, we need front-room churches, restaurant churches, store-front churches, ecumenical parties , frontier ministries, group ministries, mission agencies, community houses and whatever else the ingenuity of small groups can get going." (TJT p51).

But this was all some twenty five years ago. We may well feel such enthusiasms have had their day. However, SICEM's Lopham Street church, which back in the early eighties asked itself the question; "What kind of churches
 Would be people's churches
 In the inner city?"
finds itself today metamorphosed into the Furnival pub-cum-community church.

The Cross

Only after seeking to be faithful to all the previous gospel patterns of the Jesus-event does it become appropriate for us to approach the cross and to consider its implications for our discipleship. When John asserts that "... in the New Testament, the cross of Jesus is to be seen as secondary to his whole life, rather than his whole life as secondary to the cross." (SC p150) we are talking here in terms of sequence and not of significance. The one could not have occurred without the other and by its nature is a secondary, or subsequent event.

Nor can it be understood without the whole sequence of previous gospel patterns being in place, the clue to which John suggests is "self-sacrifice":

"The crucifixion is not, therefore, something the Church `glories in', except in so far as it is prepared to have its own sufferings and allow them also to be `glory'." (TJTp52)

An illustration of how genuine involvement in the self-giving of the cross requires immersion in the totality of the gospel pattern is to be found in the story of the sale of the Grimesthorpe church to the New Testament Church of God.

"On Friday, 22 September 1978, Grace walked in to Wesley Hall, with the children for Sunday School. When they went through the kitchen door, they got on to the stage, and saw great swastikas daubed on the walls, the piano overturned and `NF' painted on it, and on the floor, the slogan
Wogs, Go Home...
National Front slogans and racist and obscene signs were everywhere.

The next morning,... we went round together, murmuring `No! It cannot be', `Who would do such things?' Then we sat down on the front forms, and tried to pray, but only tears came." (ITC p98).

Without being there, without responding to their need, without sharing in their witness there could have be no meaningful sharing in the pain of a church community so publicly abused. The cross comes as the culmination of all that goes before. But it is not the last word.

Resurrection

In what sense can we claim the resurrection as one of those gospel patterns arising from the historical secular world? Ironically it is only when the resurrection event is treated as a literal historical event, on a par with, say the crucifixion, that any problem arises. If, however, it is understood as an expression of the church's ongoing faith, as "...the `Yes' of God to the life of incarnation, healing, identification, forgiveness, discipleship and crucifixion." (TJT p55) then its place within the historical world is clear.

"Negatively, the resurrection has to be rescued from personal salvation piety." (TJT p55). Nor is this simply a matter of challenge to the individual Christian but to the wider church community which all too often celebrates the Easter joy without recognising that it "...can only live `in the spirit of the resurrection' by living the whole Jesus mystery through again and again." (TJT p56).

Celebration of this Easter joy in the inner-city situation is necessarily a more muted event, but probably more genuine for all that;

> "Is it ever Easter in the inner-city?...Not everything is raised... But Jesus things are raised... If we want to know what or who is raised, we must look for what or who has been crucified.. the incarnate, the healer, the parabler, the actor of parables, the caller of disciples, the embodier of kingdom, the exposer of powers, the forgiver of victimisers...So take courage, There's going to be no new revelation. The revelation has already happened. Now it's all clear (almost!). Go back and tell them. And, next time, witness and act as if you know it! And tell it all again, the way it really is!" (ITC pp.105-7)

Parousia

Paousia is "Holding all things together".

> "Christianity is the claim this kind of pattern of existence, summarized in incarnation, healing, hiddenness, crucifixion, and resurrection, holds the whole universe, the whole cosmos together." (SC p156)

>> (1) All things are made by Christ
>> (2) All people are found in him
>> (3) All things hold together in him
>> (4) All things find their end in him
>> (5) All things are yours.

These "five 'alls'" (SC 156ff) become the starting points for discovering "the exciting possibilities for a theology of God's action in history which would be completely based on the actions of God in Christ:"
(1) points to "the new being of humanity foreshadowed in Jesus, differentiating itself from all attempts to abandon Christology for mere humanism".
(2) points to "the 'new morality' of the kingdom, differentiating itself from all bogus 'new moralities'."
(3) points to "the hidden presence of the issues of discipleship within secular situations, differentiating itself from all theories of mere 'progress'"

(4) points to "the way whereby the techniques of identification and crucifixion operate, differentiating itself from either 'mere expediency' or 'pure witness'."

(5) points to "the actual pattern of existence 'in Christ,' differentiating itself from theories of Christian discipleship based purely on either vicariousness or mysticism." (SC, pp227-8)

These "exciting possibilities" have proved to be the basis of John's ongoing ministry and we are thankful for it in so far as it has stimulated and challenged our own thinking and doing. It is a ministry based on the conviction that "Christianity is the claim that 'the things of Jesus' are the only ultimate things; that everything is 'held together' by them; that whatever God there is, is a God who supports them; that whatever truth there is, is truth 'as it is in Jesus';..." (TJT p57).

* * * * * * *

Hopefully in this overview I have managed to convey, in broad outline, John's "plan to relate the whole pattern of Christ to the whole of human life and history" (SC p207).

No doubt we will all have our own points of agreement and divergence. While finding the overall argument convincing that "Theology must work from Christology, for the claim of Christianity is, that... Jesus is the clue to existence and to whatever God there is and to whatever worlds there are or are to be." (SC p199), I would still wish to make a critique on some matters of detail. These concerns cover both the content and process of the gospel patterns themselves and a desire for a clearer understanding of the Christ dynamic that makes them happen.

In the list of gospel patterns that we have covered there would appear to be some important omissions, some uncertain inclusions and a question concerning the sequence itself.

Let us consider the matter of omissions first.

Beginning with Incarnation, John's scheme moves immediately to a "healing ministry". This would seem to me to beg the important question of how it is that we move from a passive static condition of being in a given context to wanting to do something about it. And what are the details of the process through which we must go?

In my paper "Patterns of the Kingdom - Hermeneutical Circles in Luke and Acts" I suggest that there are several important steps in the sequence between these to moments , without which the overall pattern loses its coherence. They are as follows:
1. Decision/Baptism (Lk2:1-7) - moving from passive recognition to pro-active commitment to Kingdom change
2. Confusion/Temptation (Lk4:14-22) - outlining the content and direction of mission in the light of Kingdom values
3. Collaboration/Discipling (Lk5:1-11) - making allies in the collegial task of Kingdom building
4. Tradition/ Spirituality (Lk16:16-17) - drawing strength from the biblical heritage.

These supplementary stages, or something like them, help us to bridge the gap between simply being there and responding to need with a healing ministry. They also help us realise what a challenging and demanding process this is. (The question about what it might be that empowers us in the chrysalitic transformation we shall consider anon.) While recognising this gap in John's scheme it needs to be pointed out that some of these categories are mentioned as sub-headings in his chapter on "Healings" (ITC 19ff).

Then there is the question of the order in which the sequence moves. Although this broadly follows the narrative of Jesus' life as we have it in the gospels, there are points where it is helpful to make some adjustments. For instance, in John's scheme not only does the 'healing ministry' follow on immediately from 'incarnation', it also precedes the 'disciple group' moment. Without wanting to sound too pedantic it can be argued that the discipling process, the making of allies, is more properly to be located as part of the preparatory process of Jesus' ministry which is essentially collaborative in nature.

Thirdly I'm not convinced that the inclusion of 'parables' and 'acted parables' is appropriate to a scheme which seeks to outline the gospel patterns of the "Jesus-event". John refers to them at one point as "evangelistic strategies" and this would appear to be a more appropriate understanding of their role. Strategies are the means by which a goal is achieved and no doubt in the ministry of Jesus both these methods were important. But as we have suggested strategies have their time and for one reason or another are used or not as the case may be.

With some such modifications to John's original scheme a more complete sequence of gospel events making up the gospel pattern can be recognised, as I have developed in my paper, "Patterns of the Kingdom."

1. Incarnation
2. Baptism   10. Pentecost
3. Temptation   9. Resurrection
4. Mission Statement 8. Passion
5. Discipling   7. Ministry
6. Spirituality

This sequence in turn has the quality of a hermeneutical circle which, starting from the given reality of 'incarnation' re-interprets that reality in the light of the gospel reality. The several 'moments' we have been describing relate to the new pentecostal reality. Behind all this is the powerful Christ "dynamic" which remains shrouded in somewhat opaque language;

"It is impossible to separate Jesus from earthly actions, whether or not they have this power (dynamis). It is also impossible to separate this power from the actions of the secular Jesus. We are not therefore dealing with a 'separated' power when we talk of a dynamic Christology. We are talking of the deeds of the secular Jesus." (SC p187)

John would appear to be suggesting that the gospel dynamic lays within the workings of the hermeneutical circle of gospel patterns itself and that it is no added extra from beyond. For the power which ensures that the interpretive process moves round and spirals into God's future, we need look no further that the process itself. But where in particular?

In his book, **Jesus before Christianity**, Albert Nolan constantly refers to the central role of compassion in the gospel narrative;

"It is not necessary to speculate about Jesus' psychology. We know that he was moved to act and speak by a profound experience of compassion...a prophet did not only share God's knowledge, he was filled to the point of bursting with God's own feelings and emotions. In the case of Jesus it was God's feeling of compassion that possessed him and filled him..." (p124).

Within the gospel patterns we can readily identify the story of the passion with its climax of Jesus' crucifixion as the point which has moved the church to compassion from the earliest days. Like a chain reaction the gospel pattern has within itself the fission required to produce its own dynamic which continues to move each generation that is grabbed by it to respond.

We shall end with a story of John's in which he faces an unlikely group (but then aren't we all?) with the challenge of this compassion dynamic;

> "Thursday, 25 September 1980. Months before, I had agreed to go over to the western outer suburbs of Sheffield, to speak to the Probus Club, in Dore. It turned out to be the first meeting of elderly gentlemen I have ever addressed - forty-five of them: retired businessmen, teachers, tax inspectors. I gaped. I had agreed, anticipating my tenth anniversary, to speak on 'Starting Again in the Inner City'. I took a deep breath, and dived...and I told them about the Mission...".

After a coffee break John tells us;
> "Sitting at the front was a man with a question.
> 'Dr Vincent,' he said, 'What do you want?'
> I was a bit stunned by the question. But he was serious. 'I want your grandsons and your granddaughters, I said. 'I want them to change their entire way of life, their expectations of life, their style of life. And I want a few of them to come and live and work in the inner city.'
> 'Do you think people who could choose would come and work with you in the filth and depression of your area? Do you think everyone is a Jesus Christ? Do you want everyone to be a Jesus Christ?'
> 'Yes,' I gasped. 'Yes! Yes! Yes!'" (ITC 139f).

Vincent, J.J., Secular Christ (SC)
Vincent, J.J., The Jesus Thing (TJT)
Vincent, J.J., Into the City (ITC)
Nolan, A. , Jesus before Christianity, Darton, Longman and Todd, London 1976
Pagan, R., Patterns of the Kingdom, (unpublished).

POLITICS

Where is Christ? Christ is wherever his ministry is being performed. Christ is in politics when they lead in any way to his Kingdom. Christ is in economics when they manifest his healing, when they feed the hungry, clothe the naked. Christ is in the movements of people's minds, whether Christian or not, when they strive for a new internationalism, or for justice, or for peace, or for disarmament. Christ is in the call for honesty which millions today address to their politicians. Christ is in the frustration and good intention of the Christians - including the Councils of Churches! - when they agonize over the right thing to do. Christ is in the facts of our age - in nuclear power, in our modern "materialism", in the needs of strategic jobs, in the opportunities for service and leadership.

Christ is there.

We can be with him or against him. We can look for him or be blind to him.

The choice is ours.

<u>Christ in a Nuclear World</u>, 1962, p.160

The enterprise of setting up a socialist State was always understood to be a project which would serve the working class ... Alongside this, however, another element was always present. It was the moral case for an equal society, the crusade to set up such a society, and the compassion and comradeship that such lifelong commitments generated ....

So let us start proclaiming some new visions for the future which will be bold and significant enough to justify some radical personal change and some radical personal commitment. And for those already committed, there's more. Can a movement survive unless there are some visible and dramatic instances of its proposals, visible in the public arena for all to see? A *movement needs not only people and a vision. It needs also miniature examples of what it is talking about and fighting for. In a time of no consensus, there is work to be done setting up some twenty-first-century garden villages, Port Sunlights, Moravian settlements and Villages in the City. Radical communities in which Christian commonness and socialism can be demonstrated as practical economic and social realities might have to precede any new agreement that a socialist or communitarian system for the nation can again be worked towards. And the histories of both Christian movements and socialist movements suggest that setting up alternative communities is part of the strategy for getting a lever on the future.*

"Jesus as Politician", 1993, pp.87-88

A POLITICAL CHRIST?

ALAN BILLINGS

John Vincent is one of the few remaining examples of a rare breed, well on the way to becoming an extinct species: the egalitarian Christian socialist. He believes that the creation of an equal (socialist) society is necessary if the poor are to be delivered from poverty and marginalisation; that the Bible commits Christians to work for such a society, not least because Jesus did; and that as a first step the people of God need to create small examples of what a larger socialist society might look like. I have come to believe that this analysis and agenda lacks credibility. Instead, I will suggest that we need to learn some rather different lessons from the churches of the poor, both past and present. Although I am critical of what John writes I acknowledge the debt I owe to him for his writing which has made me think and rethink many times over the years.

The end of egalitarianism

I refer to John as an "egalitarian socialist" - someone who believes that the state has both the duty and the ability to bring about greater equality between people. But is the epithet "egalitarian" really necessary? Can there be "non-egalitarian socialists"? Apparently there can. The Parliamentary Labour Party currently has over four hundred in its ranks, for New Labour is ideologically committed , as Old labour was not, to the maintenance of an *unequal* society. The post-landslide euphoria has blinded many on the left to the reality of the way the political landscape changed in 1997. The significant change has not been from Conservative to Labour but from Labour to New Labour - as the defection of Lord Rothermere to the Labour cause serves to underline. New Labour not only enthusiastically endorses the market system with its consequent inequalities, it also refuses to significantly mitigate those inequalities through the tax system. Egalitarian socialism has been abandoned; inequalities will grow and capitalism is safe in New Labour's hands.

There are various ways of interpreting this rejection of egalitarian socialism. Old Labour (such as it is) regards it as simple betrayal. Some Tories see it as Mrs Thatcher's finest hour. New Labour MPs say all they are doing is allowing traditional socialist values to find expression in ways more appropriate to the times. (The road to Westminster has been every bit as eventful as the road to Damascus). An alternative and politically more charitable view is to say that those on the political left no longer believe that the creation of a more equal society is the route to bringing the marginalised into the mainstream of society. The argument is that an equal society was never an end in itself (one can almost hear John Prescott saying it) but only a means to an end, the end being the lifting of the poor out of poverty. It is, of course, quite true that an equal society might not be a prosperous one: an equal society could be one in which all were equally poor - on the lines of Castro's Cuba. The minimal lesson of the communist phase of world history is that equality and prosperity do not necessarily go hand in hand. But many have in addition concluded that the communist experiment also tells us that equality can *never* result in prosperity and that inequality is both necessary and inevitable if economies are to grow and poverty is to be alleviated. New Labour has accepted this because no one on the left - no new Tawney - had arguments for equality which were robust enough to counter the case which the political right made under Thatcher and which seemed to be so powerfully borne out by the collapse of communism. It is worth briefly rehearsing the anti-egalitarian case.

Inequality is inevitable. In any given society, even if people start off with roughly the same income and wealth, the same family, social and educational backgrounds, they quickly become unequal. This person decides to squander everything in immediate consumption, whereas this one invests for long-term gain. These two risk all on some speculative ventures, one is successful and the other not. This person takes on additional work, this person is feckless and workshy. This person enjoys good health all her working life, whereas this person is dogged by an illness which makes it impossible for him to hold down any job for any length of time. Of course people do not start off from a position of equality, but even here, if we wanted to make a level playing field, the crucial factor is almost certainly something beyond the capacity of governments to influence: intellectual ability. Evidence from the USA strongly suggests that how well people do in their lives is crucially linked to their intelligence. In a free society and a world subject to change and chance, inequalities result all the time from the exercise of free choices as well as simple good or bad fortune. Governments could only prevent inequalities developing if they assumed draconian powers and exercised them constantly - which is unthinkable in a democratic state.

Inequality is inevitable. It is also necessary. Economies only grow if enterprise and the entrepreneurial spirit is rewarded. Why otherwise should someone take those risks which have to be taken if new businesses and so new jobs are to be created or new products or services developed? If hard work and taking risks result in the entrepreneur enjoying the same standard of living as the feckless, why bother? It is true that people can be motivated by rewards that are not material - the satisfaction of doing a job well, or doing something creative, or exercising power. They can also act altruistically. Most of us probably work for a mixed bag of motives, but material self-interest is usually a factor for most of us at least some of the time and for some people it may be the primary motive in their working at all. There will always be some jobs in any economy and under any system which require the incentive of a pay packet to persuade to do them at all. How else shall we get our septic tanks emptied? In other words, if the moral argument for equality is that it is the way to raise up the poor, it has been countered by a more powerful moral argument for inequality: the pursuit of equality leads to a general impoverishment in which the poor are dragged down even further; the pursuit of inequality leads to a general raising of living standards for all, including the poor.

One reason for John becoming part of a rare breed, therefore, is that the egalitarian socialist has been losing the argument badly throughout the Thatcher years - or rather, the Thatcherites have been winning a debate in the absence of any serious challenge to the type of arguments I have set out and in the light of the material and moral bankruptcy of former socialist societies. There is now no Thatcherite nostrum which Gordon Brown and John Prescott are not capable of absorbing into the new synthesis. (The road to Hull is paved with them). But if the important thing is that the poor are helped out of their poverty and the idea of an equal society was only a means to that end, does it matter if the egalitarian route is abandoned in favour of a better-run and more productive economy from which all will benefit (the once derided "on a rising tide all ships float" or "trickle down" theories)?

A risky strategy

If this is what the Labour Party is seeking to do, it is a high risk strategy. Historically, it has not been altruism on the part of the rich so much as fear of revolution and then socialism that has been the most potent factor in persuading capitalism to check its own excesses and have a regard for the poor. Socialist parties did not always have to take power in order to exercise influence - though the possibility of their taking power had to be a reality. Accordingly we have seen across Europe restraints on capitalism and the creation and acceptance of welfare states on the part of governments of all political shades. In Britain, the Labour Party built the welfare sate on the pioneering work of pre-war Liberals and the Conservatives consolidated and extended it. On the continent it has often been Christian Democrats or their equivalent that have sustained welfare capitalism. Even in the United States of America, where the threat of a socialist party has never really existed, the fear of world communism has acted as a spur to both Republican and Democratic Administrations seeking some measure of redistribution away from the better off towards the poor. The collapse of communism in the east and the wholesale abandonment of egalitarian socialism by left-wing parties elsewhere has created a wholly new political situation whose eventual outcome cannot be foreseen. But from the perspective of an egalitarian socialist these are anxious times. At the very moment when egalitarians should be rejoicing - with the Labour landslide of 1997 - they have to face a harsh truth: this was their moment of final defeat; no one in British politics today is seriously seeking to build an equal society because no one feels the moral case for it. Indeed, they feel rather the moral case for inequality.

The rhetoric of social justice

And there is more. The idea of an equal society was underpinned by the notion of social justice. The idea that poverty is the result of injustice is a key element in the egalitarian socialist argument. This was why the (old) Labour Party, which was committed to a more equal society, when it set up its enquiry into poverty, called it a Social Justice Commission. The party recognised that an equal society would require a redistribution of resources and any attempt to redistribute resources compulsorily from one group of people (the better off) to another (the poor) would require compelling moral justification. Otherwise, to adapt Proudhon, socialism would be theft. The moral case is that poverty is the result of injustice and therefore compulsory redistribution is not theft but fairness, a righting of wrongs.

(It is worth noting that the concept of social justice is one of those aerosol terms which are sprayed in order to leave a lingering fragrance rather than say anything precisely. Egalitarian socialists employ it with the idea of equality in mind; but non-egalitarians also use it to give moral justification to shifting resources to the poor. The term is extensively used by New Labour because it suggests a commitment to the poor without entailing any decisive shift towards an equal society. From the standpoint of Old Labour the language is more fig-leaf than blue print).

The Thatcherite critique of the concept of social justice, however, has been just as severe as the critique of equality and it too has gone largely unanswered. Again, it is worth reminding ourselves of some of those criticisms since they reveal that the idea of social justice is too insecure a basis on which to build policies and programmes for the future.

First, there is the critique of the idea that poverty is the result of the exploitation of one group of people by another. Within each country, the socialist argues, there is class exploitation, between countries there is the exploitation of colonialism, across the world there is the exploitation of global capitalism. But poverty is not always, and perhaps not often, the result of one group of people acting unjustly towards another. Some countries, for instance, may be poor as a result of having few natural resources or because they are periodically ravaged by flood or famine. Their poverty is not the result of injustice - no on else in the world is inflicting this upon them. This is a matter of misfortune. Again, countries may be poor as a result of a culture of laziness - manana - or because they keep tearing themselves apart in civil wars. Their poverty is no one's fault but their own. Similarly with social groups within countries. Poverty may result from misfortune or be self-inflicted. It makes little sense calling this "injustice", though much poverty may result and many innocent ones - such as children or dependent relatives - may suffer.

It might, of course, be argued that when we speak of "injustice" in these circumstances there is no suggestion that someone or some group has created an unjust situation; it is being suggested rather that a situation of comparative disadvantage exists and the disadvantaged have a right to have their disadvantage removed. It is the idea of "rights" which justifies governments taking resources from one group of people and giving them to another even though the first group has not actually caused the misfortune of the second. But it is a most extraordinary state of affairs. We live in a world of comparative disadvantages of every conceivable kind. Does this create rights for disadvantaged groups and duties on governments to secure redress in every case? The people of Cumbria do not enjoy the same amount of sunshine per annum as the people of Kent. Does this create a right on the part of the people of Cumbria for - if sunshine cannot be delivered - some sort of compensation at the expense of the people of Kent which the government has a duty to secure? Who is to say? Of course, the people of Kent may feel sorry for the people of Cumbria, and may be moved to do something for them. But that is a matter of one group responding to the needs of another out of a spirit of generosity. It is not a matter of a third party - the government - being justified in intervening in order to secure someone's rights. (A further effect of seeing all inequalities as instances of injustice is that each time we put one injustice right we are liable to create others! If the government compensates the people of Cumbria for their lack of sunshine, they are put immediately into a more favourable position than the people of Dumfries who similarly lack sunshine.) The idea of social justice begins to fall apart as soon as we try to be specific.

This leads to the second point. If many, perhaps most, instances of poverty are not the result of injustice, this does not alter the fact that there are poor people in the world and they have some basic needs. If their needs are to be met, appeal must be made on a different basis. Historically, in the Christian west this has been done in two ways: encouraging self-help on the part of the poor and charity or philanthropy on the part of the rich. But once poverty is understood in all circumstances as injustice, self-improvement is not attempted and charity and philanthropy are treated with contempt. If people have rights, self help and generosity do not enter the frame; only justice will do and that requires the action of a third party (government) to bring it about. The danger of speaking about all situations of inequality in the language of social justice is that we create and perpetuate dependency cultures in which the well-springs of compassion and gratitude and the spirit of self-improvement dry up in equal measure.

But what about the Bible?

But the *Christian* egalitarian socialist might reply that the Bible commits him or her to speak about social justice. Here I must declare my own hand and begin to posit alternative ways forward. Does the Bible speak of social justice? The answer is almost certainly not. The rhetoric of social justice is not Biblical but comes out of Enlightenment theories of human rights which have played such a large part in the development of the legal systems of liberal democracies. This, rather than the Bible, is the true context of the idea of social justice. The word the Old Testament prophets used, sedakah, is sometimes translated as "justice" and thus assimilated to the idea of social justice, but it is better translated as righteousness and applied to a much wider area of life. The prophets wanted people to behave in every area of life righteously. In the economic sphere this meant, amongst other things, dealing honestly with people and not exploiting the poor. It did not carry any sense that poverty was always the result of the exploitation of one group by another.

Nor can we speak of Jesus as politician. It is, of course, true that his mission brought him into conflict with both religious and political leaders, not least because in his day the religious leaders also played a political role. But to suggest that Jesus had a political agenda is to make him into some first century Ayatollah - though one who went about it in a particularly crass manner. One of the differences between Christianity and Islam is that Christianity carries with it no idea of the Christian states to be imposed on all people once political power is achieved - though this has been denied by Christians as diverse as egalitarian socialists and members of the Dutch Reformed Church of South Africa. Christianity was able to be midwife at the birth of the liberal state. and Christians can exist happily within it in a way which Islam will always find difficult.

The Bible is not, then, the source of the idea of social justice and Christians are not called upon to respond to people in need on that basis. This is just as well since, as we have seen, many instances of need are not the result of injustice. Moreover, if we were to treat people in need on the basis of justice, some needs might never be met at all. What is the just response to the child abuser? He clearly has great needs; his only hope is that we do not treat him according to justice. A different basis of response is necessary if certain needs are to be met. Here we must recall the gospel. Surely we have not forgotten the witness of Paul and Luther and Wesley that God does not deal with us on the basis of justice? The gospel is about God's generosity towards us - his charity. This is the basis of God's dealing with us and the Christian foundation for acting in the world. And this is the lesson that we learn from the poor themselves.

Learning from the churches of the poor

Let me here interject a brief autobiographical note. A few years ago I went under the auspices of the Urban Theology Unit to study at the New York Theological Seminary. One evening, I was taken to meet members of a congregation of Hispanic Protestants in Brooklyn. They were immigrants, surviving in the main on poverty wages in down-town Dickensian garment factories. They dared not organise or complain about conditions since they risked immediate dismissal, and, in the case of the illegal immigrants, deportation. But poverty in New York is preferable to near starvation in Latin America. I joined a small group for their mid-week worship. It was in Spanish - but I hardly needed an interpreter to understand the way the Christian Gospel was empowering them. They were Pentecostals. They sang, some spoke in tongues, they read the Bible together, they discussed their lives in the light of what they read, they prayed, they planned action. It was impossible to be present at their meeting and not be overwhelmed by their vitality and the sense of the Holy Spirit's presence. After the worship they took me to another part of the building where several hundred people - from teenage to eighty - were learning English. An ability to speak good English was, they were sure, the key to getting on - and they were determined to lift themselves out of poverty by their own efforts - or rather, with the direct help of the Spirit.

This type of Pentecostal Christianity is sweeping through Latin America (and elsewhere), changing the consciousness and so altering the lives of countless millions of poor people. It is a profoundly liberation form of Christianity. Those who believe that we have lessons to learn from the poor must take their own advice and hear what these people are saying to the churches.

The religious presuppositions of this type of Christianity can be simply stated and ought to come as no surprise to those who come out of the evangelical tradition. First, the dignity and worth of each individual is powerfully affirmed through the assurance that he or she is the object of God's saving grace. Whatever evaluation the city government,. the employer, the police or the landlord might make of them, they knew their real worth as people for whom Christ died. Moreover, they need not be weighed down by past sins and failures for Christ died precisely in order to win for them forgiveness and the possibility of a fresh start. Second, as a result of that, they were called upon to take full responsibility for their lives under God. Married couples were to cherish one another and bring up their children well. Everyone was expected to work hard, to be honest and generous in all their dealings and to respect one another. Third, they know they could do none of these things without superhuman help. God gave them the one resource they needed for their struggles - the Holy Spirit. And the same Holy Spirit would pour out upon them all the gifts they needed to build up congregations of Christian people.

This underlying theology and the direct experience of the Spirit in worship gave these poor people astonishing confidence. Victims became agents - the goal of all liberation theology. They wanted to tell me how this man had stopped beating his wife and become a model husband and father, how this old woman had first learnt to speak English herself and was now teaching these young men all she knew; how this man, who had once been on drugs, had been promoted at work because he was so reliable and trustworthy. All this had been done by the power of God; they knew they could do none of these things in their own strength. Lives were being radically transformed by the Holy Spirit - not just for the duration of a campaign against the local authority, but permanently.

What do we say about this? In sociological terms, what we see happening in these poor churches is the building up of social capital - cultural resources which gradually have an impact on the wider life of the community. These poor Hispanic Americans are being empowered and will certainly lift many in the next generation if not their own out of poverty. There is nothing new in this. It is the history of early Christianity. It is the history of early Methodism. In addition, they are providing precisely the small-scale examples that John Vincent wants of how the wider society could be. But these small scale examples are not communities or enterprises standing over against the church, they are the church. This is what each local congregation is - the small scale example, the place of counter culture.

What I came to realise in New York was that so often, Liberation Theologies, in not pointing to the activity and power of the Holy Spirit in the local church, are reductionist just at the point where the gospel holds out the possibility of life-changing transformation and through it the accumulation of social capital. Contrary to what we thought in the 1960's and 1970's - that Christianity needed to be secularised if it were to be relevant to the needs of the poor - these poor churches were witnessing to the fact the Christianity is at its most powerful when it is at its most religious.

MISSION

The Question, Did Jesus found the Church? can only be answered by taking it to the New Testament. But to take it there means to expose ourselves to a completely different kind of Church from the Church which exists anywhere today.

The Church of the New Testament is a radical Church. If had to be. It could not have arisen except for radical, curious, highly singular reasons. It could not have endured but by having distinctive, radical and questionable understandings of existence and rules of life which would only commend themselves to those who took the same stance of "faith in Jesus Christ".

It is often stated that the birthday of the Church is Pentecost. I believe that the Church, the ecclesia, began as soon as Jesus began "calling out" people to be his followers and giving them his commandments for discipleship. This "calling out" took place wherever the demands of Jesus were heard and in any sense understood. Almost everything he did with the twelve - his teaching them to memorise his words, his "acted parables" for them, his depicting their life or apprenticeship and servanthood in terms which he used also of his own - suggests that he envisaged that the discipleship that they were learning from him would be of continuing significance after his death. But it was the element of discipleship to him as Master and Lord which was to be of lasting value. The human ecclesia, or chosen group, was constituted alone by its common obedience to him. The Church was "Christ's". It was his people, his disciples, his brothers and sisters, his "fellow-heirs". Without him, it would never have been. With him, it could not do otherwise than "exist". And "exist" in a highly peculiar, radical ways, simply because it was his, and they were his disciples.

The Working Christ, 1968, pp.7-8

THE CHRIST OF URBAN MISSION

COLIN MARCHANT

Who is this Christ?
What does He ask of us?

Two questions, asked and answered in Sheffield, echoed and etched in East London. The answer - He is here and He is real.

1. HE IS HERE.

He is here, tangled up in the details, rooted in the realities. Another John told us, "In the beginning ... the word became flesh and dwelt among us". The Sheffield John spells it out ... "the first dynamic of Christ, the dynamic of incarnation". Right at the start of <u>Strategies for Mission</u> it is flagged up ...

"The gospel of incarnation is always about what happens "at the bottom". God in Christ is not content to shed his glory, but takes the very bottom place of society. Being found in fashion as a man, Jesus becomes a servant, a very slave of humanity, and even becomes condemned and crucified. Jesus says that the Lord is to be as a servant." (<u>Strategies for Mission</u>, p.2)

This Christ is born under an inn, lives in the streets, goes to the towns and the cities of His day. He is to be found now where the litter blows and the paint peels, in the inner cities and housing estates as well as the suburbs and cathedral towns. He is part of, rooted in, belonging to .. in the flesh, he is here in time, place and experience. He is where the people live and the crowds gather.

Such an awkward Christ, so uncomfortable to those who carry His name haunts us as we slide out to the suburbs, or flee like lemmings to the coast - a silent and shaming commentary on our motives and our methods. A constant call back to the first principle of Mission - Christ's and ours - incarnation.

Years ago I heard a Frenchman, Jacques Ellul, saying it in his <u>Presence of the Kingdom</u>.

When we really understood the actual plight of our contemporaries, when we have heard their cry of anguish, and when we have understood why they won't have anything to do with our "disembodied" Gospel, when we have shared their sufferings, both physical and spiritual, in their despair and their desolation, when we become one with the people of our nation and of the universal church, as Moses and Jeremiah were one with their own people, as Jesus identifies Himself with the wandering crowds, "sheep without a shepherd, THEN we shall be able to proclaim the Word of God - but not till then."

Constantly and continually I have heard the same steady beat from John and Grace Vincent in Sheffield. Begin here!

2. HE IS REAL.

"The most significant discovery in theology in my lifetime has been, to me, the rediscovery of Jesus as a real person in history, and the re-assertion of obedience to Jesus along the lines of the Synoptic Gospels, as over against the Catholic and Protestant belief systems along the lines of Paul ..."

So writes John in his piece in <u>Twenty Twenty Visions</u> (p.67). We could cross swords on the cavalier disposal of Paul, but join hands on the shout for a real Jesus!

The Christ of Urban Mission is real.

How real can you get? Birth and death, bread and wine, money and work, homes and journeys, friends and enemies .. places and people, hurt and hope.

How unreal we have made Him ... frozen in stained glass windows, lifted out by our liturgies, misted over by our sentimentality, trapped in our privatised religion, codified in theology.

He is real, forever puncturing the wheels of our escapism or refusing to accept the spiritualisation that dilutes the reality.

This is the Christ who gave us the manifesto of Luke 4:

> to bring good news to the poor .....
> to proclaim liberty to the captives
> and recovery of sight to the blind
> to set free the oppressed
> and announce that the time has come.

This is the Jesus who touched lepers, welcomed children, walked with women, argued with the religious, fed the hungry and spoke directly.

He's for real, man!

After our questions and His answers come the requests (or is it commands?). He asks of us what He asked of Himself. To be there - and to be real. To work it out for ourselves, to make it real for others in the here and now - and to keep the vision. That I have heard from - and seen in - the place called Sheffield and the man called John.

3. EARTH THAT GOSPEL

If incarnation is the primary theological note, earthing is the pragmatic consequence. For John, that earthing of the Gospel has to be in a place - Sheffield for him, East London for me. Where is it for you? And that local earthing has to be worked out in the here and now. In buildings, whether church or pub; in policies that become the programmes, in people - whether local action or group training.

In <u>A Community Called Ashram</u> you will find a summary of a group-response:

1. Be the place where the Kingdom is proclaimed and in parts lived out.
2. Be the Community following Jesus, which could be normal church or para-church.
3. Be the place where Christian discipleship in radical forms is found by individuals.
4. Be small supportive challenging groups networking and learning from each other.
5. Be a place of conflict between institutional Church and alternative Communities.
6. Be the place of celebrating the bits of hope and healing in the world.

(<u>A Community Called Ashram</u>, p.8)

In the models of ministry and the networks of association the Vincent commitment has been to the earthing and extension of the Gospel. The evidence of action is there - in the wider acronyms ... MAP, COSPEC, NACCAN - Mission Alongside the Poor; Christian Organised for Social, Political and Economic Change; National

Association of Christian Communities and Networks. All wrestling, with John in there, with being authentic and appropriate in today's urban world.

4. KEEP THE VISION

Anyone who can put "Love Divine" and "The Red Flag" together knows something about dreams, hopes and vision! Set in <u>Hymns of the City</u> (now reprinting) are two Vincent "gems". Membership of the Church and the Christian Socialist Movement is his earthing and embodying of vision - spiritual and/or political.

"Yours the movement for empowering
Yours the Kingdom, sure and meek,
Yours the banquet for our flowering
Yours the shalom cities seek
Ours your faithful love upholding
Ours your grace outpassing fears
Ours the mystery unfolding -
Christ who wipes away all tears!"

(Tune: Love Divine .... Blaenwern)

His Kingdom makes our hopes arise;
All shall be free, and good, and wise,
All will their heavenly fulness bear,
All will have riches, all will share.

Then raise his scarlet standard high,
Beneath its folds we'll live and die
Though cowards flinch and traitors sneer
We'll keep Christ's red flag flying here.

Let's join his movement, grasp his hand
See tiny foretastes in our land,
Here let his Commonwealth begin!
Let's give and share, and let all in.

(Tune: The Red Flag ... Tannenbaum. The Chorus is Jim Connell's original "Red Flag" plus only "Christ's")

Many of us share the Vincent vision. While John was the Methodist President I became the Baptist President with "Shalom" as my theme and message. That "shalom" for all ... individual wholeness, oneness in relationships, embodied in congregations, sought in the communities and cities and covering the plant .. a Biblical vision carried by Jesus, the "Prince of Shalom". I can sing with him "yours the shalom cities seek". And I see his hand in the latest of his contributions from the Methodist Church and NCH Action for Children, <u>The Cities, a Methodist Report</u>.

There is in part 5 of <u>The Cities</u>, a summary of "a vision for Britain's cities"
>The pursuit of prosperity
>a more socially just society
>a greater sense of personal security
>a cleaner, more sustainable city environment
>a greater sense of community
>an enhanced Church's role in community life.

Towards the end of 1996 I travelled home from Nairobi with John. We were returning from the first World Congress on Urban Mission. John now carries a new brief - joint chair of Urban Theologians International. In that, as in previous chapters, we will catch again the authentic notes of incarnation and reality. From that, we will continue to hear the Christ of Urban Mission calling us to earth His Gospel and to keep the vision.

The Christ of Urban Mission ...
Who is this Christ?
What does He ask of us?

JOHN JAMES VINCENT

BIBLIOGRAPHY

1955
"The Evangelism of Jesus", Journal of Bible and Religion, October, reprinted in Witness to the Campus, ed. R Ortmayer, Methodist Student Movement USA.
"Evangelism and Discipleship", Motive, Meth.St.Mvt. USA, October

1956
"The Mystery of Discipleship", The Student Movement, March

1957
"Didactic Kerygma in the Synoptic Gospels", Scottish Journal of Theology, September

1959
"The Parables of Jesus as Self-Revelation", Texte und Untersuchungen, Akademie-Verlag, Berlin: Studia Evangelica I

1960
"Discipleship and Synoptic Studies", Theologische Zeitschrift, Basel, December

1961
"The Methodism Gone Forever and the Methodism Striving to Be Born", four articles, Methodist Recorder, September

1962
Christ in a Nuclear World, Crux Press, also Fellowship Publications USA
"Living Without the Bomb", Frontier, Winter

1963
Christ and our Stewardship: Six Bible Studies, Epworth Press,
"Christ's Ministry and our Discipleship", Biblical Realism Confronts the Nation, ed. Paul Peachey, Fellowship Press.
"Theology and Nuclear Politics", Frontier, Summer

1964
Christian Nuclear Perspective, Epworth Press.
Ground for Meeting, Rochdale Methodist Mission
"Did Jesus Teach his Disciples to Learn by Heart?", Texte und Untersuchungen, Akademie-Verlag, Berlin: Studia Evangelica III
"The Christian as Layman and Minister", Preacher's Quarterly, July and September
"Markus", "Markusevangelium", "Nachfolge", "Mysterium", Biblisch-Historisches Handworterbuch, Vandenhoeck & Ruprecht, Gottingen

"New Bottles or New Wine?", London Quarterly & Holborn Review, October
"The Realism of Jesus Christ", The Friend, 8 May, pp 566-568; 15 May, pp 591-592

1965

Christ and Methodism: Towards a New Christianity for a New Age, Epworth Press. Also Abingdon Press.
"Reply to John Robinson", Prism, June, pp 31-34
"Oscar Cullmann", Expository Times, October, pp 4-8
"New Morality or New Discipleship?", New Directions, Autumn

1966

"Between Protest and Politics", Peace on Earth: The Way Ahead, ed. Walter Stein. Sheed and Ward
"Oscar Cullmann", in Theologians of Our Time, ed. AW Hastings. T&T Clark (Reprint of article)
"Secularisation", Study Encounter, Vol 2.1
"After 'Christ and Methodism'", Methodist Magazine, January
"Prayer for the Modern Man", The Livingstonian, South Africa, Vol.1. No.6

1967

Here I Stand: The Faith of a Radical, Epworth Press
"Town Centre Stand", Methodist Home Mission Report, 1966-67
"What Shall we do with the Church?", New Directions, Summer
"Theological Prospects for Radicals", Christian Action, December

1968

Secular Christ: A Contemporary Interpretation of Jesus. Lutterworth Press. Also Abingdon Press.
The Working Christ: Christ's Ministries through His Church in the New Testament and in the Modern City, Epworth Press.
"Christocentric Radicalism", Christian Century, 8 May
"Good Seed: Stony Ground?", Beware the Church, ed. JW Waterhouse, Epworth Press
"Radical Christianity", Kingsway, West London Mission, Summer
"More than a Humanist", New Christian, 8 August.

1969

The Race Race, SCM Press. Also Friendship Press.
"A New Kind of Existence for Others", Breakthrough, January
"Beginning with Jesus", New Christian, 10 July, 28 August
"God - in the Christian Sense", Christian Century, 10 September

1970

"A Renaissance for Theology through Racism?", Christian Advocate, 30 April
"Urban Theology", The Month, December

1971
Pitsmoor for Tomorrow, editor and contributor, Pitsmoor Action Group. Urban Theology Unit.
"Christology as Secular Dynamic", Christian Century, 24 March
"Some Hesitations on Hope", Religion in Life, Spring
"From Unity to Multiformity", Frontier, May

1972
Ministry in Cities, editor. Urban Theology Unit, Summer
"Theological Education for Today", Theology-Action Training, New City 2
"A Strategy for Radicals", New Christian, March
"Playing God for the City", The Human City, New City 3, Summer

1973
The Jesus Thing. Epworth Press. Also Abingdon Press.
Towards the Future Church, editor. New City 5, Spring
"Doing Theology Today", Study Encounter, 41, Vol. IX No. 2
"The Disciples in Mark", SNTS Conference Papers, September
"Innovation in Great Britain - the Sheffield Urban Theology Unit", Learning in Context, Theological Education Fund, World Council of Churches; also in Ministry Between Today and Tomorrow, New City 7/8
"Messianism and Pluralism", Christian Renewal, Spring

1974
"The Para-Church - An Affirmation of New Testament Theologies", Study Encounter, 55
"What is Happening", Epworth Review, January
"Search for Stories", Search for Gospel, New City, 6

1975
New Wine, New Wineskins, editor. New City, 9
"SICEM", One for Christian Renewal, March
"Alternative Planning", and "An Alternative County", South Yorkshire in Search of a Soul, New City, 10
"The Para-Church", Towards Renewal, No 4, Autumn
"A Family Communion", Worship and Preaching, April, Vol.5. No. 2

1976
Disciple and Lord: The Historical and Theological Significance of Discipleship in the Synoptic Gospels, Academy Press, (revised Basel DTheol. 1960 dissertation)
Stirrings: Essays Christian and Radical (editor and contributor). Epworth Press.
Alternative Church, Christian Journals
"Christians and the Old Testament", Epworth Review, May
"Mealtime Eucharist: New Testament and Today", Worship and Preaching, June

"Alternative Theological Education", Doing Theology in the City, New City, 11
"Christian Theology and the Challenges of Our Times", (The first Carl Michalson Lecture) Drew Gateway, Winter. Reprinted as Alternative Journeys, 1981.
"Proposals for the Church", Methodist Recorder, 10 October

1977
Strategies for Mission, Urban Theology Unit.
Community Worship, ACT 14.
"Strategies for Mission", Epworth Review, May

1978
"Pluralism and Mission in the New Testament", Studia Biblica, Volume III

1979
Alternative Theological Education (editor and contributor), Urban Theology Unit.
Festival for the Future Church, ACT 18.
"Wholeness and Gospel", The Whole Community, ACT 19.
"Finding Good News in the City", Crucible, April-June; also in Backyard Seminary, New City 13, 1981
"Sheffield - One Way", Living in Hope, Methodist Home Mission Report 123
"Doing Political Theology", Drew Gateway, Winter, Vol. 50. No.2

1980
Inner City Issues (with Roy Crowder), Liverpool Institute of Socio-Religious Studies.
"Doing Theology", Agenda for Prophets, ed. R Ambler and D Haslam, Bowerdean Press, reprint of "Doing Political Theology".
"Basic Communities in Britain", Putting Theology to Work ed. Derek Winter, British Council of Churches
"Theological Education in the 80's in Britain: Adaptation or Alternatives?", Ministerial Formation, April
"Welcome to the new life of old Sheffield", Reform, April
"A Call to Christians Everywhere", Working Together, ACT 20
"Inner City Politics for Christians", Christian Action Journal, Autumn. COSPEC issue.

1981
Starting All Over Again, World Council of Churches.
Alternative Journeys, Urban Theology Unit.
Two Nations: One Gospel? (contributor) Methodist Home Mission/UTU.

1982
Into the City, Epworth Press.

"Discipleship - A New Way of Living", Bible Studies, Worship and Preaching, February, April, June, September
"What we are Learning", COSPEC Stories, SCM publications.
"I have a Dream", Methodist Home Mission Annual Report, 1981-2

1983
"Towards an Urban Theology", New Blackfriars, January
"Working with Parables Today", Gospel Starters, ACT 21
"Urban Theology: A Liberation/Bondage Theology for Britain", Society for the Study of Theology, Oxford, 3-6 April

1984
OK Let's Be Methodists, Epworth Press.
Gospel from the Poor (editor and contributor), Methodist Home Mission/UTU.
"Urban Training: A Plea for Priority", Christian Action Journal, April
"Travelling on in Ashram Community", ACT 22
"Living with the Gospels Today", City Forum, Oxford, September
"What is the Gospel?" Gospel from the Poor, New City, 16
"Theological Education for Urban Mission", Ministerial Formation, August
"Mission Alongside the Poor - Thoughts and Resources" 3 articles, Methodist Recorder, January

1985
Radical Jesus Manifesto (joint author) ACT 23
"Dialogue between Rich and Poor", Epworth Review, September
"What on Earth is Jesus For?", Methodist Recorder, 4 February
"Basic Christian Communities in Britain", Churches Register, Autumn

1986
Radical Jesus, Marshall Pickering.
Mark at Work (with John D Davies), Bible Reading Fellowship.
"TSB: The New Future" TSB Depositors Association, June
"Where We Are is Who We Are", Grassroots, March-April
"Images of God and Discipleship", The Way, October

1987
Community Worship, Rev. Ed. (editor), ACT 25.
"Poverty: the Churches' Task", Christian Action Journal, Spring
"Mission and the Kingdom", What it Means to Me, ed. David Bridge, Methodist Home Mission Division

1988
"The Political Mission of Jesus", Society for the Study of Theology, Leeds, April

1989
Five Pillars of Christianity, Urban Theology Unit, (Methodist Presidential Address).
Britain in the 90's, Methodist Publishing House.

Hymns of the City, editor, Urban Theology Unit.
"James", *Guidelines*, Bible Reading Fellowship
"Faith and Ministry in Divided Britain", *Methodist Recorder*, 26 January
Articles as President of the Methodist Conference, June 1989-June 1990, *Methodist Recorder*

1990

Gospel in the 90's, Methodist Publishing House.
"Open Letter", *Dear Next Prime Minister*, ed. Neil Astley, Bloodaxe Books

1991

Discipleship in the 90's, Methodist Publishing House.
"Mark's Gospel in the Inner City", *The Bible and the Politics of Exegesis: Essays in Honour of Norman K. Gottwald*, ed. David Jobling, Peggy Day and Gerald Sheppard; Cleveland: Pilgrim Press
"Is Health the Same as Wholeness?" *Health and Wholeness*, ACT 27

1992

Liberation Theology from the Inner City, Urban Theology Unit.
A Community Called Ashram, (editor and contributor) ACT 28.
"Racism and Theology: a Perspective from a British Inner City", *Report of the Chantilly Pan-European Consultations*, Geneva: Programme to Combat Racism, World Council of Churches
"Christian Politics and Discipleship", *Religion in Public Life*, ed. Dan Cohn-Sherbok and David McLellan; London: St Martin's Press
"People's Church: Christianity as a Movement of the Poor" *20/20 Visions: the Futures of Christianity in Britain*, ed. Haddon Willmer, London: SPCK
"Liberation Theology and the Practice of Ministry", *Southwell and Oxford Papers on Contemporary Society*, Oxford: Oxford Institute for Church and Society

1993

A Petition of Distress from the Cities, (joint author and editor) Urban Theology Unit.
"Jesus as Politician" *Reclaiming the Ground*, John Smith and Others: Tawney Lectures; London: Hodder & Stoughton
"Sixties Theology Today" *Methodist Recorder,* 9 December

1994

Good News in Britain: Five Bible Studies, Urban Theology Unit.
Por La Vida, (joint author), Colombia Civil Rights Delegation Report, Justice and Peace Commission, Liverpool.
"Personal Experience", *Glimpses of God*, ed. Dan Cohn-Sherbok; London: Duckworth

"Bonhoeffer: Building Theology and Discipleship", <u>Bonhoeffer and Bradford: 60 Years On</u>, ed. David J. Moore; Milton Keynes: Church of Cornerstone

"Angry Young Man", <u>No More Mr Nice Guy</u>, Birmingham: Student Christian Movement

"The Vocation and Significance of UTU", 25th Anniversary Lecture. Urban Theology Unit.

"Radicalism of Jesus", <u>Methodist Recorder</u>, 3 November

"Option for the Poor", <u>Methodist Recorder</u>, 24 November

"Training for Ministry at the Urban Theology Unit", <u>British Journal of Theological Education</u>, 1994-95 No 3 Winter

1995

<u>Liberation Theology UK</u> joint editor with Chris Rowland, Urban Theology Unit. Vol 1 of series, <u>British Liberation Theology.</u>

"Liberation Theology in Britain, 1970-1995", in <u>Liberation Theology UK.</u>

"Sheffield: Die Hoffnung muss von unten wachsen", <u>Der Uberblick</u>, March

"What are we waiting for? Liberation Theology Politics", <u>Christian Socialist</u>, Summer

"Discipleship in Mark", <u>Cliff Today</u>, Autumn

"Tony Blair - Speaking up for us All", <u>Christian Socialist</u>, Winter

"Remnant Theology as the Base for Urban Ministry", in <u>Signs of Hope in the City</u>, ed. R Linthicum, MARC, California

1996

"Interview" on Liberation Theology, with Gareth Jones. <u>Reviews in Religion and Theology</u>, 3, August

"Imaginative Identification", <u>Epworth Review</u>, 3, September

"Ordination Training for Public Life", <u>Christians in Public Life Papers</u>, 15, Birmingham

"History of the City as Formative in its Development", International Urban Ministry Congress, Nairobi, November

"Christmas on our Street", 4 articles, <u>Methodist Recorder</u>, Nov 29, Dec 6, 13, 20

1997

<u>The Cities: A Methodist Report</u>, joint chair with Helen Dent, NCH Action for Children.

<u>The Cities Workbook</u>, editor, NCH Action for Children

<u>Faith from the City</u> (joint editor with Chris Rowland), Urban Theology Unit. Vol 2 of series, <u>British Liberation Theology.</u>

"The Challenges and Responsibilities of Contextual Theology," <u>Reviews in Religion and Theology.</u> 1, February

"The Gospel Agenda in Great Britain", <u>City Cries</u>, 34

"An Inner City Learning Community", <u>The Way</u>, April

Other Articles

British Weekly, 1955-65
Methodist Recorder, 1960-
New City, editor, Urban Theology Unit, 1970-97
ACT, editor, Ashram Community Trust, 1980-
"Face to Faith", **The Guardian**:
   World Recession and the Eighties (2 Feb 80), City Lights (3 Feb 86) Margaret Thatcher and John Wesley (19 Oct 87), A Fresh Start for Hope (28 Dec 87), A Chill has Settled on Wesley's Warm Heart of Methodism (23 May 88), Why the Begging Bowls are out for Care Schemes (24 Oct 88), Reasoning and the Resurrection (3 Apr 89), Digging up Radical and Earthy Church Traditions (8 Aug 92), Cycle of Schism is what comes Naturally (24 Oct 92), Between the Bishop and the Virgin (19 Dec 92), Upside Down in the Kingdom of God (26 Feb 94)

Book Reviews in: **Theologische Zeitschrift** (Basel), **British Weekly**, **New Christian**, **Methodist Recorder**, **Epworth Review**, **Drew Gateway**, **Modern Believing**.

BIOGRAPHY

Posts Held:

Minister, Manchester and Salford Mission, 1956-62
Superintendent Minister, Rochdale Mission, 1962-69
Methodist Superintendent, Sheffield Inner City Ecumenical Mission,
   1970 - 1997
Visiting Professor of Theology,
   Boston University School of Theology, Autumn 1969
   New York Theological Seminary, Spring 1970
   Drew University, Theological School, Spring 1978
Director, Urban Theology Unit, Sheffield. 1969-97; Director Emeritus,
   Core Staff Member and Supervisor MPhil/PhD, 1997-

Part-time Appointments include:

Extra-mural Lecturer in Theology, Manchester University, 1966-69,
   Birmingham and Leeds Universities, 1971-75
Visiting Lecturer, St Paul School of Theology, Kansas City, July 1968
Rall Lecturer, Garrett Theological Seminary, Illinois April 1969
Supervisor, Sheffield University Biblical Studies Dept./UTU
   MPhil/PhD in Contextual, Urban and Liberation Theologies, 1993-

Honorary Appointments include:

Elected Member, Studiorum Novi Testamenti Societas, 1961
Lecturer, Oxford Congresses on New Testament, 1957, 1961, 1965
Member, Oxford Institute for Methodist Theological Studies, 1962,
   1967, 1972, 1977, 1982, 1987, 1992
Secretary, Regional Working Party, World Council of Churches
   Commission on Defence and Disarmament, 1963-65; 1969-72
Member, Theological Commission, Christian Peace Conference,
   Prague, 1965-69
North-West Vice President, Campaign for Nuclear Disarmament,
   1957-69
Founding Member, Editor, Methodist Renewal Group, 1961-70
Founding Member, Leader, Ashram Community Trust, 1967-
Founding Joint-Chair, Alliance of Radical Methodists, 1970-74
Founding Member, Council, Christian Organisations for Social,
   Political and Economic Change, 1980-90
President, Methodist Conference of Great Britain, 1989-90
Honorary Lecturer, Biblical Studies Dept., Sheffield University, 1990-
Co-ordinator, British Liberation Theology Project, 1991-96
Steering Committee, International Urban Mission Network, 1991-
Joint Chair, Urban Theologians International, 1991-
Member of Human Rights Delegation to Colombia, May 1994
Director, Institute for British Liberation Theology, 1996 -
Co-Chair, Methodist Working Party on the Cities, 1996-7

UTU PUBLICATIONS

NEW CITY JOURNAL

18.	UTU in the 80s	£2.00
19.	A Petition of Distress from the Cities	£1.00

NEW CITY SPECIALS

1.	John Vincent	Strategies for Mission	.20p
2.	Consultation	Alternative Theological Education	£1.00
3.	John Vincent	Alternative Journeys	.60p
4.	Ed Kessler	Radical Jesus in Parables	.50p
5.	Marian Lowndes	A Mission in the City	£1.00
6.	John Vincent	Hymns of the City	£1.00
7.	John Vincent	Five Pillars of Christianity	.60p
8.	Margaret Walsh	Here's Hoping	£2.00
9.	John Vincent	Liberation Theology from the Inner City	£1.00
10.	Laurie Green	God in the Inner City	£2.00
11.	James Ashdown	Gentrification	£2.00
12.	Laurie Green	Jubilee	£2.00

PEOPLE'S BIBLE STUDIES

1.	Ed Kessler	The Good Samaritan	£2.00
2.	John Vincent	Good News in Britain	£1.00
3.	Ed Kessler	Lost & Found & Overpaid	£2.00

BRITISH LIBERATION THEOLOGY

Edited by Chris Rowland and John Vincent

1.	Liberation Theology UK	£7.50
2.	Faith from the City	£7.50

Please add postage: £0.40 plus £0.15 per £1 over £1.00 order.
Send cheque payable to Urban Theology Unit
to UTU, 210 Abbeyfield Road, Sheffield S4 7AZ